Copyright Notice

CCNA v3 Routing and Switching: Exam Study Notes

Copyright © 2017 Shaun L. Hummel

Disclaimer

This book was written as a study guide to Cisco CCNA certification. While every effort has been made to make this book as accurate as possible no warranty is implied. The author shall not be liable or responsible for any loss or damage arising from the information contained in this book.

About The Author

Shaun Hummel is a Senior Network Engineer with 15 years enterprise network planning, design and implementation experience. He works for various public and private companies in Canada and the United States improving infrastructure, security and network management. Author of *CCNA v3 Routing and Switching 200-125*.

Contents

Introduction

CCNA v3 Routing and Switching: Exam Study Notes is a technical summary guide for CCNA candidates. It is based on the top-rated book *CCNA v3 Routing and Switching: 200-125*. There are 300+ study notes included with concepts, key points and IOS commands designed for review of all CCNA exam topics. It effectively consolidates CCNA v3 training from books, courses and lab guides.

There is coverage of *all* new and updated CCNA topics based on official CCNA v3 exam guidelines. New topics include IPv6 addressing, GRE, QoS, MPLS, MLPPP, PPPoE, eBGP, SDN and APIC-EM. In addition there is coverage of switch chassis aggregation, firewalls, wireless devices, cloud services, virtualization, port-based authentication and DHCP snooping. Exam study notes are a key part of your training strategy for passing ICND1 100-105, ICND2 200-105 and 200-125 exams.

CCNA Test Strategies

- ✓ Subnetting is a key aspect of the CCNA exam for both theoretical and lab simulation questions. It is easy as well to make mistakes when converting between binary and decimal values. Write all class B and class C subnets on paper when the exam starts. Include the number of hosts available per subnet and conversion charts.

- ✓ Don't burn time with a question you could only guess on. Take your best guess and move on to the next question.

- ✓ Take some practice tests that are 90 minutes long to verify you are scoring at least 80% and have honed your time management skills properly. It is helpful to practice complex questions with show commands and drawings.

- ✓ Do not waste time considering your answers from previous questions.

- ✓ Take your time with SIM questions. Verify the answers carefully noting any syntax or configuration errors missed or not included before submitting. Do not click *Next* until you have answered each question.

- ✓ Complex questions are sometimes comprised of convoluted wording, drawings and show command listings. Consider fundamentally what the question is testing.

- ✓ Make notes when going through CCNA books and labs to summarize key points, rules and commands for exam day review. For example OSPF require various settings to match for neighbor connectivity. In addition the wrong wildcard mask won't advertise the correct subnet range to neighbors.

✓ Read each question a couple of times carefully. Note the subtleties with each question that Cisco employs and what the question is really asking. The following is an example of wording for a CCNA style question.

How do you verify that an interface is operational (up/up) and responding?

    A. show interfaces

    B. show ip interface brief

    C. telnet

    D. ping

The key word **responding** is used here and that implies sending a packet to an interface and verifying the packet returns.

A. The command *show interfaces* is wrong. You are at the device so cannot verify connectivity and send/return of echo messages.
B. The command *show ip interface* brief is wrong. You are at the device so cannot verify connectivity and send/return of echo messages.
C. Telnet is wrong. Device requires a Telnet configuration. You would not know if the problem was with the Telnet configuration (application layer) or the interface (Layer 3).
D. Ping is the best answer. The ICMP packet is sent to the interface and returns with either destination unreachable or packets received to confirm the interface is operational.

✓ There are four SIM labs worth 30% - 35% of all exam points. The following are recommended guidelines for managing time.

- 4 SIM labs x 12 minutes per SIM = 48 minutes
- 40 multiple choice = 32 minutes
- 6-10 other question types = 10 minutes

1.0 Network Fundamentals

1.1 <u>Compare and Contrast OSI and TCP/IP Models</u>

The following describe the network services at each layer of the OSI model. Each lower OSI layer provided services to the next higher layer. Effective troubleshooting should start from the physical layer and verify connectivity to the application layer.

Table 1-1 OSI Layer and Network Services

application layer	network services to applications
presentation layer	data formatting, translation, encryption, encoding
session layer	logical communication between host processes
transport layer	windowing, error recovery, segmentation, reliability
network layer	logical addressing, routing and path selection
data link layer	framing, media access control, layer 2 MAC addressing
physical layer	putting binary bits on physical media, electrical signaling

Protocol Data Unit (PDU)

The Protocol Data Unit (PDU) is based on the headers added as data is encapsulated from the application layer data to the physical layer. The encapsulation process adds a header at each layer.

Layer 1 = bits, Layer 2 = frames, Layer 3 = packets, Layer 4 = segments

OSI Model Data Encapsulation

Each lower layer adds a header to the PDU from the next upper layer

- Segment encapsulates data from all upper layers (5-7)
- Packet encapsulates transport layer segment
- Frame encapsulates network layer packets
- Physical layer converts all to binary bits for transmission across the wire

The *data link layer* creates a frame with source and destination MAC address along with control information. The *network layer* creates a packet with IP addressing and control information. The *transport layer* divides a data stream into segments. Reliability and flow control information is added when the transport protocol is TCP

TCP/IP Reference Model

The newer TCP/IP model is based on the popularity of TCP with internet connectivity and network applications. TCP/IP model is the industry standard for network connectivity. The TCP/IP model integrates the OSI model session layer, presentation layer and application layer into a single application layer.

TCP/IP Model   **OSI Model**

- Application Layer = Session, Presentation and Application Layer

- Transport Layer = Transport Layer

- Internet Layer = Network Layer

- Network Layer = Physical Layer, Data Link Layer

1.2 Compare and Contrast TCP and UDP Protocols

The transport layer provides reliable host-to-host peering connectivity with TCP or UDP protocols. TCP is connection-oriented with handshake setup, flow control and sequencing. The purpose of error recovery and retransmission is to detect, prevent and correct packet drops. It is less efficient than UDP with increased overhead and packet processing.

UDP is faster than TCP however it is connectionless with no guarantee of packet delivery (best effort) and error detection only. The CRC/FCS checksum from the frame is checked and any UDP datagrams that have errors are discarded. Some applications such as video streaming prefer UDP where there is less latency resulting from retransmissions.

Table 1-2 TCP/UDP Port Assignment

Telnet	TCP 23
SMTP	TCP 25
FTP	TCP 21
HTTP	TCP 80
SNMP	UDP 161
DNS	TCP/UDP 53
HTTPS	TCP 443
SSH	TCP 22
TFTP	UDP 69

Inter-Application Communication

The session ID provides logical communication for each application process. It is at the OSI session layer where there is session setup and tear down. Each file download session for instance is assigned a unique session ID. The FTP download and web browser are separate applications that are each assigned a unique session ID.

The port number or socket number identifies each application running on the same server. The server distinguishes where to forward arriving packets for each application based on port number.

1.3 Describe the Impact of Infrastructure Components in the Enterprise

The firewall can inspect packets up to the application (layer 7). The only layer 3 device is the router however firewalls can provide routing services as well. The switch, wireless access point, wireless LAN controller and bridge are all layer 2 devices.

Table 1-3 Network Devices and OSI Layer

firewall	layer 7
wireless access point	layer 2
wireless LAN controller	layer 2
switch	layer 2
router	layer 3
bridge	layer 2

Broadcast and Collision Domains

Layer 2 network devices create a single broadcast domain (VLAN) with the initial default configuration. Assigning VLANs creates a broadcast domain for each VLAN. Routers and firewalls create a single broadcast domain per interface. Collision domains are created on each full-duplex Ethernet interface. For example, a switch with 48 ports create 48 separate collision domains however the uplink to the router is only a single collision domain. Wireless access points are half-duplex media that share a single collision domain among multiple wireless clients. There is however a single collision domain on the switch uplink.

- router with two switches connected = 2 collision domains
- wireless access point connected to a switch = single collision domain
- switch interface connected to router = single collision domain
- switch VLAN = single broadcast domain
- 48 port switch = 48 collision domains (1 per port)
- wireless access point with 100 clients = single collision domain

Example 1:

Refer to the network drawing. Each Gigabit switch port is a single collision domain. There are 72 Gigabit Ethernet switch ports including 3 uplinks that create a maximum 75 available collision domains. There is a default VLAN 1 on each switch that defines a single broadcast domain between switches. In addition there is a separate broadcast domain for each router interface. The network topology defines 3 broadcast domains and 75 collision domains.

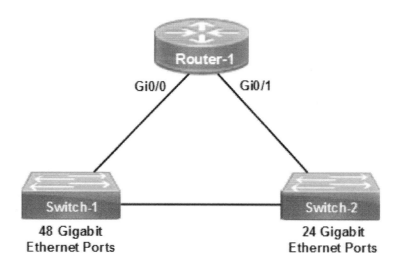

Wireless Access Point

The wireless access point is essentially a bridge where packets arrive and are forwarded based on MAC address. The access point however is a single broadcast domain with a shared collision domain.

The wireless RF cell is half-duplex media with CSMA/CA required for collision detection. There is a wired side of an access point with an Ethernet port uplink to a switch. The access point is similar to a desktop or IP phone where PortFast is enabled.

- wireless client transmits signal based on standards support (802.11a/b/g/n)
- 802.11b/g clients cannot connect to 802.11a access points
- 802.11a clients cannot connect to 802.11b/g access points
- 802.11n clients can connect to 802.11a/b/g/n access points
- 802.11a/b/g/n clients can connect to 802.11n access points
- nearest access point that supports wireless standard (802.11a/b/g/n) responds

Wireless LAN Controller

The wireless LAN controller (WLC) is a layer 2 network device. The purpose of WLC is to manage wireless access points. It does not route packets however it does rewrite layer 2 frame header between wireless 802.11n and Ethernet format. The source and destination MAC address are updated as well.

14

The following are primary characteristics of wireless LAN controllers:

- Layer 2
- DHCP relay
- Frame switching
- STP node
- Proxy ARP

Advantages of wireless LAN controllers

- enable easier management and deployment of access points
- enable configuration of wireless user policies across the network
- dynamic RF management

1.4 Describe the Effects of Cloud Resources on Network Architecture

The cloud is essentially an internet based service enabling connectivity from any device and from any location. The three primary traffic flows include the following:

Data Center Backhaul

Backhauling traffic from branch offices and customers is available. The traffic is routed through the data center DMZ and forwarded over direct links to the cloud. This topology often increases network latency and utilization on the internet routers.

Point-to-Point

Broadband point-to-point connectivity between branch offices and cloud. This is becoming the de facto standard for branch office connectivity. The DSL provides internet access for direct connectivity to cloud services.

Multipoint

Multipoint connectivity between data center routers and cloud. The internet routers at the data center are hubs for multiple WAN links to the same or different cloud services. It is effective in that each link is a direct point-to-point connection. Redundancy is available as well for failover to a secondary cloud service.

Virtualization Components

The primary components of a virtualized solution include hypervisor, virtual machine (VM) and server hardware. The number of virtual machines (VM) that can be supported on a single server is based on memory, CPU, switch uplink speed and hard disk space

1. **Hypervisor** manages requests from virtual machines for server hardware. The hypervisor abstracts (separates) the hardware layer from operating system. That enables applications and operating system software to run on any hardware platform.

2. **Virtual Machine (VM)** is a virtual server with bundled applications and operating systems. Sends requests to hypervisor for hardware services. The virtual appliances (switch, firewall etc.) are network services bundled as a VM.

3. **Server** hardware includes CPU, memory, hard drive and network interface card.

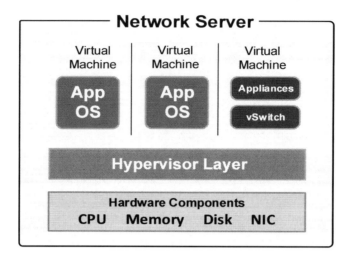

The five primary characteristics of cloud computing architecture:

- resource pooling
- elastic capacity
- metered billing
- multi-tenancy
- anywhere access

Standard network services available from cloud service providers:

- redundancy
- VPN encryption
- SAN storage

Three primary services of the virtualization model:

- network access control
- tenant segmentation
- virtual machines (VM)

Cisco network virtualization model includes tenant segmentation, security policies and virtual machines. Tenant traffic is segmented with various techniques for path isolation. Network access is managed with security policies and virtualized network services are based on virtual machines (VM).

16

Virtualization Advantages

The primary advantages of virtualization include cost effectiveness, faster deployment, optimal hardware utilization and network management.

Cost Effective - fewer physical servers are required for the same number of applications. Less data center cabling, power and cooling is required.

Faster Deployment - virtual machines make deployment faster with bundled application that can be copied, distributed and activated when required. Virtualization enables easier disaster recovery as well with virtual machines.

Optimized Hardware Usage - server hardware is utilized at much higher rates with multiple virtual machines. That is preferable to physical servers staying idle when a single application is deployed.

Network Management - virtual servers (VMs) are abstracted from hardware making them agile, easier to manage and assign to servers. The network performance provided by virtualization is a disadvantage. The virtualized environment is a shared infrastructure model. There is often some increased network latency and less throughput than with a physical server. Encryption is available with physical and virtual servers as a network service.

1.5 Compare and Contrast Collapsed Core and Three-Tier Architectures

The traditional Cisco network design model is comprised of three distinct layers. Each layer provides network services for performance, redundancy, security and scalability.

- access layer
- distribution layer
- core layer

The new Cisco architecture promotes a collapsed core architecture. The collapsed core is comprised of an access layer and a core layer. The distribution layer is collapsed into the core layer along with associated services.

Collapsing (combining) the distribution layer and core layer into a single core layer requires fewer network devices and uplinks. The Layer 2 topology is simplified and STP issues have less effect on the switching infrastructure. It isn't as scalable as the 3-tier model making it preferable for smaller data centers.

- easier management
- layer 2 optimization
- cost effective

1.6 Compare and Contrast Network Topologies

Star Topology

The star topology or sometimes called hub and spoke is a point-to-point connection between multiple endpoints and a hub. It is most often deployed for connecting smaller branch offices to a hub or data center. There is no link redundancy making it the most cost effective.

Partial Mesh Topology

The partial mesh has at least two paths to a single or multiple upstream neighbor endpoint/s. It provides more link redundancy than the star topology along with increased cost. The hybrid topology is a customized solution comprised of at least two different topology types. For instance combining a partial mesh topology with a star topology.

Full Mesh Topology

The full mesh topology is referred to as any-to-any connectivity. It is characterized by a link that connects a single endpoint and all neighbor endpoints. It provides the maximum redundancy and is the most expensive. It is often deployed for connecting multiple data centers or where maximum link redundancy is required.

1.7 Select Appropriate Cabling Type Based on Requirements

- straight-through cable = connect dissimilar network devices (switch to router)
- rollover cable = console port
- crossover cable = connect same class devices (switch to switch)
- serial cable = WAN interface (DTE/DCE)

Table 1-4 Ethernet Standards

1000Base-LX/LH	Single-mode Fiber (SMF), 1000 Mbps, 10 km
1000Base-SX	Multi-mode Fiber (MMF), 1000 Mbps, 220 m - 550 m
Cat 5	Copper, 100 Mbps, 100 m
Cat 5e	Copper, 1000 Mbps, 100 m
Cat 6	Copper, 10 Gbps, 55 m
1000Base-LX	Multi-mode Fiber (MMF), 1000 Mbps, 550 m
1000Base-ZX	Single-mode Fiber (SMF), 1000 Mbps, 70 km

1.8 Apply Troubleshooting Methodologies to Resolve Problems

The following describes the standard Cisco recommended troubleshooting methodology. The minimum recommended time to escalate the incident is after all information has been collected.

>Step 1: Identify problem
>
>Step 2: Collect information
>
>Step 3: Analyze data
>
>Step 4: Eliminate causes not relevant
>
>Step 5: Propose hypothesis
>
>Step 6: Verify with test plan
>
>Step 7: Solve problem

1.9 Configure, Verify and Troubleshoot IPv4 Addressing and Subnetting

It is important to understand how to convert from IPv4 decimal notation to binary for subnetting and summarization.

- The binary system is based on ones (1) and zeros (0).
- There are 8 bits per octet, 4 octets per IPv4 address.
- The bit value is based on position.
- The bit set to 1 sets the value. The bit set to zero = 0
- There are 8 bits with 2 (nth power) so 2^8 = 255
- Per octet: set all bits to 1 = 255, set all bits to 0 = 0

0	0	0	0	0	0	0	0	= 0
1	1	1	1	1	1	1	1	= 255
8	7	6	5	4	3	2	1	bit position
128	64	32	16	8	4	2	1	bit value

Binary to Decimal Conversion

Converting binary number to an equivalent decimal number requires adding the values of each bit position set to (1) for each octet. The sum of each octet creates a dotted decimal value (IP address).

0 0 0 0 **1** 0 **1** 0 = 10

from right to left, 2nd bit = 2 and 4th bit = 8 = 2+8 = 10

Binary to Decimal Conversion

Converting the binary number to an equivalent decimal number requires adding the values of each bit position set to (1) for each octet. The sum of each octet creates a dotted decimal value (IP address).

00001010.01100100.00101000.10000000

(8+2) . (64+32+4) . (32+8) . 128 = 10.100.40.128

Decimal to Binary Conversion

Converting IPv4 address 192.168.64.10 to an equivalent binary number requires setting specific bits for each octet to (1) value. The sum of each octet must add up to the decimal value for each octet.

192 . 168 . 64 . 10

11000000 . 10101000 . 01000000 . 00001010

(128+64) . (128+32+8) . 64 . (8+2)

Hexadecimal to Binary Conversion

IPv6 addressing is based on hexidecimal format instead of IPv4 octets. The IPv6 address is comprised of 32 hexidecimal values of 4 bits each. The IPv6 address is as a result 128 bits in length (4 bits x 32 hexidecimal values). Each hexidecimal number has 16 possible values that range from 0 to F derived from the lower 4 bits of an octet. The same values from 0-9 are used for IPv4 and IPv6 binary to decimal conversion. The values 10 to 15 however are A to F.

Hexidecimal D = 1 1 0 1

8 4 0 1 = 8 + 4 + 1 = 13 decimal

Hexidecimal F = 1 1 1 1

8 4 2 1 = 8 + 4 + 2 + 1 = 15 decimal

A = 10 (1010)
B = 11 (1011)
C = 12 (1100)
D = 13 (1101)
E = 14 (1110)
F = 15 (1111)

Converting FDA4 to binary = 1111 1101 1010 0100

F   D   A   4

20

IPv4 Address Classes

The following are the assignable classes for global IPv4 address space. The address range from 127.0.0.0 – 127.255.255.255 is reserved for host-based loopback address.

Class A = 255.0.0.0 (0.0.0.0 - 127.255.255.255)

Class B = 255.255.0.0 (128.0.0.0 - 191.255.255.255)

Class C = 255.255.255.0 (192.0.0.0 - 223.255.255.255)

Class D = 224.0.0.0 - 239.255.255.255 (multicast)

Class E = 240.0.0.0 - 255.255.255.255 (reserved)

Private IPv4 Addressing (RFC 1918)

RFC 1918 defines private IP address space from each address class. The private IP addressing is not public routable across the internet. The standard practice is for companies to assign private addressing to all inside hosts. NAT is deployed at the internet edge where private addresses are translated to public routable addresses. The following are the RFC 1918 private IP address ranges:

10.0.0.0 - 10.255.255.255 /8

172.16.0.0 - 172.31.255.255 /12

192.168.0.0 - 192.168.255.255 /16

Classful Subnet Mask

Classful subnet masks are based on the default mask length for each IP class. That includes Class A = /8, Class B = /16 and Class C = /24. Any routing protocol that only supports classful subnet masks must use the default for the address class deployed. The default subnet mask implies subnetting is not configured for an address class.

Class A = 255.0.0.0 (/8)

Class B = 255.255.0.0 (/16)

Class C = 255.255.255.0 (/24)

Classless Subnet Mask

Classless subnet masks are referred to as variable length subnet mask (VLSM). They are any subnet mask that is not the default for a particular address class. They enable more specific routes to a destination. In addition subnetting is enabled to optimize available address space. The network portion of an IP address is shifted to the right or left. That changes the subnet mask length and enable subnetting. The number of subnets and host assignments available is based on the subnet mask length.

Example Subnet Masks:

255.0.0.0 = classful (default class A subnet mask)

255.255.224.0 = classless

255.255.255.248 = classless

255.255.0.0 = classful (default class B subnet mask)

255.255.255.0 = classful (default class C subnet mask)

Table 1-5 Class C Subnetting Table

Subnet Mask	CIDR	Subnet Bits	Subnets	Host Bits	*Hosts
255.255.255.0	/24	-	-	8	254
255.255.255.128	/25	1	2	7	126
255.255.255.192	/26	2	4	6	62
255.255.255.224	/27	3	8	5	30
255.255.255.240	/28	4	16	4	14
255.255.255.248	/29	5	32	3	6
255.255.255.252	/30	6	64	2	2
255.255.255.254	/31	7	128	1	2
255.255.255.255	/32	-	-	-	host address

* The host number does not include the network address and broadcast address. They are reserved for each individual subnet and are not assignable to any hosts. For example 8 host bits = 2^8 = 256 - 2 = 254

Subnetting Example 1:

What network address would allow the maximum number of subnets for 172.16.1.0/23 with 30 hosts?

The subnet mask defines the network portion (bold) and host portion of an IP address. The subnet mask /23 (255.255.254.0) assigns 23 bits to the network portion and 9 bits to the host portion. The number of assignable hosts is 2^9 = 512 - 2.

```
                        network          | host
172.16.1.0      = 10101100.00010000.0000000 1.00000000
255.255.254.0   = 11111111.11111111.1111111 0.00000000

                        network          | host
255.255.255.224 = 11111111.11111111.11111111.111 00000
```

22

The question asked for a maximum of 30 hosts. The subnet mask is used to modify the network portion and consequently the host portion as well. Moving the subnet mask to the right will increase the network portion and decrease the host portion assignable. Assigning the rightmost 5 bits provides a maximum of 30 hosts (32 - 2). The network address and broadcast address cannot be assigned to hosts.

    decimal 32 = 5 bits = 00000000

The host portion must be decreased from 9 bits to 5 bits. That will require increasing the subnet mask from /23 to /27.

    subnet with 30 hosts = **172.16.1.0/27**

Subnetting Example 2:

What IP address is assignable to a host based on a subnet mask of 255.255.255.224

A. 192.168.32.31

B. 192.168.32.29

C. 192.168.32.0

D. 192.168.33.1

Correct Answer: B

The network address and broadcast address are not assignable to hosts. The subnet multiple starts at 0 with multiples of 32 (0, 32, 64, 96, 128, 160, 192, 224).

             network | host
11111111.11111111.11111111.111 00000
  255.   255.   255.   224

1. 4th octet is subnetted
2. subnet multiple = 256 - 224 = 32
3. network address of subnet = 192.168.32.0
4. host range = first 5 bits = 2^5 = 32 - 2 = 30 host assignments

- network address = 192.168.32.0
- host range = 192.168.32.1 - 192.168.32.30
- broadcast address = 192.168.32.31

Subnetting Example 3:

Select the correct network address and subnet mask that allows at least ten web servers (hosts) to be assigned to the same subnet?

A. 192.168.100.0 255.255.255.252

B. 192.168.100.16 255.255.255.248

C. 192.168.100.16 255.255.255.240

D. 192.168.252.16 255.255.255.252

E. 192.168.100.8 255.255.255.252

The subnet mask defines the network portion and host portion of a subnetted address. Increasing the subnet mask length will increase the number of subnets available. Creating 10 host assignments for web servers requires at least 4 host bits. That allows for 14 host assignments where network and broadcast addresses are not assignable.

2^3 = 3 host bits = 8 - 2 = 6 host assignments
2^4 = 4 host bits = 16 - 2 = 14 host assignments

network portion = 32 bits - 4 bits = 28 bits (/28)
= 255.255.255.240

```
        network (28 bits)          | host (4 bits)
11111111.11111111.11111111.1111 0000
   255.      255.      255.    240
```

The 255.255.255.240 (/28) subnet mask starts at the bit 5 of the 4th octet and has a binary value of 16. The subnets are multiples of 16 (0, 16, 32, 48 etc).

Correct Answer: **192.168.100.16/28**

Subnetting Example 4:

What is the second IP address available for host assignment from 172.33.1.64/30?

A. 172.33.1.64
B. 172.33.1.65
C. 172.33.1.66
D. 172.33.1.1

Correct Answer (C)

The IP address is a nondefault Class A address. The subnet mask defines the number of bits assigned to the network portion and host portion. The /30 subnet mask creates a network portion of 30 bits and a host portion of 2 bits. The number of host assignments available with 2 bits = 2^2 = 4. The network address and broadcast address are not assignable to hosts. As a result the number of host assignments = 4 - 2 = 2 IP addresses. The following is a list of all IP addresses for subnet 172.33.1.64/30.

- network (subnet) address = 172.33.1.64
- first assignable host IP address = 172.33.1.65
- second assignable host IP address = **172.33.1.66**
- broadcast address = 172.33.1.67

<pre>
                          network | host
172.33.1.64   = 10101100.00100001.00000001.010000 00
255.255.255.252 = 11111111.11111111.11111111.111111 00
</pre>

The rightmost bit of the subnet mask (network bits) determines the subnet multiple and where it starts. For this example, bit 3 of the 4th octet has a binary value of 4. The subnet multiple starts at 0 with multiples of 4 (0, 4, 8, 12 etc). The next available subnet is 172.33.1.68/30. Interfaces on the same router must be assigned to different subnets.

Wildcard Masks

The wildcard mask is a technique for matching specific IP address or range of IP addresses. It is used by routing protocols and access control lists (ACL) to manage routing and packet filtering.

The wildcard mask is an inverted mask where the matching IP address or range is based on 0 bits. The additional bits are set to 1 as no match required. The wildcard 0.0.0.0 is used to match a single IP address. Wildcard mask for 255.255.224.0 is 0.0.31.255 (invert the bits so zero=1 and one=0)

<pre>
11111111.11111111.111 00000.00000000 = subnet mask
00000000.00000000.000 11111.11111111 = wildcard mask
</pre>

Example 1: Classful Wildcard Mask

The following wildcard will only match on the 192.168.3.0 subnet and not match on everything else. This could be used with an ACL for instance to permit or deny a subnet. It could define a single subnet to advertise from OSPF as well.

192.168.3.0 0.0.0.255

<pre>
        192.   168.   3.   0
   11000000.10101000.00000011.00000000
   00000000.00000000.00000000.11111111 = 0.0.0.255
</pre>

Example 2: Classless Wildcard Mask

The classless wildcard can filter based on any network boundary. The following wildcard mask matches on the subnet 192.168.4.0 serial link only. It is the equivalent of 255.255.255.252 subnet mask.

          192.   168.   4.   0
    11000000.10101000.00000100.00000000
    00000000.00000000.00000000.000000**11** = 0.0.0.3

192.168.4.0 0.0.0.3 = match on 192.168.4.1 and 192.168.4.2

The CIDR notation denotes the number of bits in the subnet mask. For instance a class C address with subnet mask 255.255.255.240 = /28

Summarization

Refer to the network topology drawing and select the IP address that will summarize all of the routes advertised to Router-1?

Summarization aggregates (includes) all bits that are common to all IP addresses. The example has four different IP addresses with /24 subnet mask. Start from the left and move right until the bits are mismatched (non-common). The common bits all occur up to and including bit 29. That translates to a /29 subnet mask (255.255.255.248) assigning 29 bits to the network portion. The /29 subnet mask can summarize IP address range 172.16.1.0 - 172.16.1.7

172.16.1.2/24 = **10101100.00010000.00000001.00000** 010
172.16.1.3/24 = **10101100.00010000.00000001.00000** 011
172.16.1.5/24 = **10101100.00010000.00000001.00000** 101
172.16.1.6/24 = **10101100.00010000.00000001.00000** 110

The summary address is obtained from the common bits that include all IP addresses ignoring the 3 non-common bits. The single summarized address is an aggregate that can advertise all included IP addresses.

Summary Address = **172.16.1.0/29**

1.10 Compare and Contrast IPv4 Address Types

The following describe the standard network message types. Multicasting forwards the same packet to multiple destinations providing most efficient bandwidth utilization.

Table 1-6 Network Message Types

Unicast	packet sent from a single source to a single destination
Multicast	packet sent from a single source to a destination group
Broadcast	packet sent from a single source to all hosts on a VLAN
Anycast	packet sent from a single source to nearest destination

1.11 Describe the Need for Private IPv4 Addressing

There are various advantages to private IP addressing that has enabled deployment across the enterprise network. The number of public IP addresses available has decreased over the past 10 years. They are now only assignable for internet access.

RFC 1918 private address space cannot be routed across the internet. There are thousands of private IP addresses that are mapped to a single public IP address with Network Address Translation (NAT). As a result public address space conservation is a primary advantage. The reuse of IP address space maximizes private IP addressing available to all companies. Host addresses are not advertised across the public internet for increased security. Intranet connectivity is enabled and at a lower cost than public addresses. The hosts can be deployed as well without internet connectivity.

- global address space conservation
- network security
- enables intranet connectivity
- less costly than public addresses
- assign to hosts without internet connections

1.12 Select Appropriate IPv6 Addressing Based on Requirements

The /48 network address block is a typical assignment to an enterprise network. It provides 16 bits for subnetting as part of the /64 network prefix. In addition there is a /64 (64 bits) available for host address portion. Each number or letter of an IPv6 address is a hexidecimal value comprised of 4 bits with 16 possible values from 0 to F. The subnet portion has 16 bits that can be assigned with variable subnet masks.

- IPv6 address = 2001:AD7:4312:1D34.0000:0000:0000:0001/128
- single subnet = 2001:AD7:4312:1D34::/64
- 65,535 subnets (16 bits) = 2001:AD7:4312::/48

- network prefix = 2001:AD7:4312::/48
- network prefix + subnets = 2001:AD7:4312:**00**00::/64
- host identifier = 0000:0000:0000:0000/64 - FFFF:FFFF:FFFF:FFFF/64

regions	data centers	subnets
0000	0000	0000 0000

The first 4 bits (49 - 52) can be assigned to identify regions (bold). The second group of 4 bits (53 - 56) can be assigned to identify data centers. The remaining group of 8 bits (57 - 64) are assigned to subnets for each data center.

- **regions** = /52
- data centers = /56
- data center subnets = /64

The number of regions, data centers and number of subnets per data center determine the subnets masks selected. For example with only 3 regions, the /50 subnet mask with 2 bits (49-50) would provide the required 4 region identifiers. The following IPv6 address ranges are assigned to regions, data centers and subnets per data center.

- 16 regions: 2001:AD7:4312:1000::/52 - 2001:AD7:4312:F000::/52

- 16 data centers: 2001:AD7:4312:0000::/56 - 2001:AD7:4312:0F00::/56

- data center subnets: 2001:AD7:4312:0000::/64 - 2001:AD7:4312:00FF::/64

1.13 <u>Configure, Verify and Troubleshoot IPv6 Addressing</u>

IPv6 is based on hexidecimal notation with values from number 0-9 and A to F. IPv6 addressing is comprised of 8 groups with 4 hexidecimal values of 4 bits each for 16 bits per group. The 16 bits per group x 8 groups equals 128 bits per IPv6 address.

The IPv6 address is comprised of a 64 bit network prefix and a 64 bit interface identifier. The 64 bit network prefix is comprised of a 48 bit routing prefix and 16 bit local subnet ID. The network prefix is similar to the IPv4 network address portion. The interface identifier is similar to the IPv4 host address portion. The subnet ID allows for variable length subnets that identify VLANs, departments, buildings and cities for instance. Regional Internet Registry (RIR) assigns IPv6 addresses to end users.

- multiple IPv6 addresses are assignable per interface
- hop limit is a new field of IPv6 packet is equivalent to IPv4 TTL field
- flow label field is new to IPv6 packet
- features that used broadcast messaging is now provided with multicasting

Advantages of IPv6 Addressing

- scalability
- no broadcasts
- address autoconfiguration

IPv6 Addressing Rules

- double colon :: can summarize multiple consecutive zeros for multiple groups
- only one double colon is permitted per IPv6 address
- multiple zeros in a single group can be summarized with a single zero.
- leading zeros in a single group can be deleted
- no less than 8 groups including zero groups

Any IPv6 address with less than 8 groups must have double colon to summarize consecutive zero groups.

Example 1:

What is the alternate equivalent notation for the following IPv6 address?

2001:25D3:0000:0000:009F:CD2A:0000:332E?

A. 2001:25D3:9F::CD2A:0000:332E

B. 2001:25D3:9F:CD2A:0:332E

C. 2001:25D3::9F:CD2A:0:332E

D. 2001:25D3:0:009F:CD2A:332E

The correct IPv6 address **2001:25D3::9F:CD2A:0:332E** does the following:

1. Minimizes multiple zero groups (group 3 and 4) to a double colon ::

2. Deletes leading zeros from a single group (group 5)

3. Minimizes a single group with all zeros to single zero :**0:** (group 7)

A. 2001:25D3:9F::CD2A:0000:332E
(double colon in wrong location and group 7 not summarized to single zero)

B. 2001:25D3:9F:CD2A:0:332E
(zero groups 3 and 4 removed instead of being summarized to double colon)

D. 2001:25D3:0:009F:CD2A:332E
(group 3 and group 4 should summarizes to double colon :: and not a single zero.
group 5 leading zeros were not deleted and group 7 removed instead of a single zero)

Example 2:

Select the valid IPv6 address from the following list?

A. 2001:0000:12D4::043D::1

B. 2001:1234:4567:AD:12DE:1

C. FEC0:ABCD:9WCD:0067::2A4

D. 2001:AD:654C:1234::9

Options A, B and C have features that are not valid with IPv6 addressing. The following explains the issues with each address:

Option A - has double colons :: occurring twice. The double colon is only permitted once per IPv6 address. 2001:0000:12D4::043D::1

Option B - has only 6 groups. IPv6 requires 8 groups (8 x 16 bits = 128 bits). Any IPv6 address with less than 8 groups must have double colon to summarize zero groups. 2001:1234:4567:AD:12DE:1

Option C - has an illegal value (W). IPv6 is based on hexidecimal notation with values from 0 to F hexidecimal. FEC0:ABCD:9**W**CD:0067::2A4

IPv4 to IPv6 Transition Methods

The solutions available for IPv4 to IPv6 transition include tunneling and translation.

- ISATAP Tunneling
- NAT Proxy and Translation (NAT-PT)
- Teredo Tunneling
- 6to4 Tunneling

IPv6 Duplicate Address Detection

IPv6 duplicate address detection is required on all unicast IPv6 addresses assigned to an interface. The detection starts with Stateless Address Autoconfiguration (SLAAC) assigning an IPv6 link-local address to a node. The network interface state is tentative during the detection process. The network administrator can enable duplicate address detection again by assigning a new IPv6 address.

There are a variety of IPv6 address states based on the operational status of the interface and duplicate address detection. The IPv6 address state is pending while the associated network interface is administratively down.

The following statements correctly describe what happens when a router detects an IPv6 duplicate address.

- duplicate global addresses are not used on interfaces where they are assigned.

- IPv6 packet forwarding is disabled on interface with duplicate link-local address.

- IPv6 addresses are all disabled on any interface that has a duplicate link-local address until it is resolved.

1.14 Configure and Verify IPv6 Stateless Address Auto Configuration

IPv6 makes addressing easier when autoconfiguration is enabled. There is a unique link-local address assigned automatically to the interface. Enabling SLAAC however does not send DNS server addressing to clients. The feature only provides an IP address and default gateway to clients. The following methods are available for assigning IPv6 addresses that are not static (manual) assignment.

Stateful DHCPv6

Stateful DHCPv6 is most similar to DHCPv4 for IPv4 addressing. The IPv6 client sends a broadcast request to the nearest DHCPv6 server for IP address configuration. The DHCPv6 server assigns the IPv6 address and any additional required addressing configuration such as default gateway, DNS server etc.

Stateless DHCPv6

Stateless DHCPv6 feature uses Stateless Address Autoconfiguration (SLAAC) for assigning an IPv6 address and default gateway to clients. The feature does however require a DHCPv6 server for sending a variety of additional IP configuration settings including DNS server address to clients.

Stateless Address Autoconfiguration (SLAAC)

Stateless autoconfiguration generates a unique link-local address based on *EUI-64* format. The IPv6 address is based on the network prefix sent in Router Advertisement (RA) from the local router. In addition SLAAC obtains the default gateway from Router Advertisements to configure clients. IPv6 processing is automatically enabled on an interface as soon as an IPv6 address is assigned to the interface. .

The IPv6 interface state is the status based on an autoconfiguration address request.

Tentative: address is being verified with duplicate address detection.
Valid: address can send and receive unicast traffic.
Preferred: address can send and receive unicast traffic.
Deprecated: address can send/receive unicasts though not recommended.
Invalid: address cannot be used to send or receive unicast traffic.

IPv6 Address Configuration

The following IOS command assigns a static IPv6 address to a router interface. The **ipv6 enable** command is not required when an IPv6 address is already assigned to an interface.

> router(config-if)# **ipv6 address 2001:AF42:1212:4F32::32/64**

The following IOS command enables autoconfiguration on a network interface. The IOS command **ipv6 enable** is not required.

> router(config-if)# **ipv6 address autoconfig**

Verify IPv6 Addressing

The following IOS command will show the status of an IPv6 enabled interface. That includes interface operational status, link-local address and global unicast address.

> router# **show ipv6 interface**

1.15 Compare and Contrast IPv6 Address Types

Table 1-7 IPv6 Address Types

global unicast address	internet routable with global routing prefix
multicast address	prefix FF00::/8 (send to group members)
unique local address	private global network, not internet routable, starts with FD00::/8
link-local address	mandatory, auto-configured, local subnet only, used for routing adjacency, prefix FE80::/64
loopback address	universal address, assigned to every interface, prefix ::1/128
anycast address	send to any member of a group that is nearest and available, typically default route ::/0
unspecified address	source address for initializing host, :1/128

2.0 LAN Switching Technologies

2.1 <u>Describe and Verify Switching Concepts</u>

The following is a list of network services provided by switches:

- switches forward data link layer traffic
- switches create and maintain the MAC address table
- switches support segmenting collision domains

MAC Address Table

Every network device is assigned a unique hardware address from the manufacturer called a MAC address. The purpose of a MAC address is to provide a unique layer 2 identifier. That enables communication between devices of the same network segment (VLAN) or different segments. The switch forwarding decisions are based on the MAC address and assigned port.

- enable packet forwarding between hosts on the same VLAN
- globally unique network device identifier associated with a VLAN

The MAC (physical) address is 48 bits of hexidecimal numbering. The first 24 bits is a manufacturer OUI and the last 24 bits (bold) is a unique serial number (SN).

OUI | **SN**
0000.00**0a.aaaa**

The switch builds a MAC address table comprised of MAC address, switch port and VLAN membership for each connected host. The switch creates a separate MAC address table for each configured VLAN. Any unicast flooding of a frame to learn a MAC address is for the assigned VLAN only.

The following IOS show command will list the contents of the MAC address table for a switch. Where there are multiple VLANs configured, the switch will list all MAC address tables for all VLANs in a single table listing. The switch builds and maintains a separate MAC address table for each VLAN configured.

switch# **show mac address-table**

Microsegmentation

The newer Ethernet Gigabit switch ports that support full-duplex operation have enabled microsegmentation. That eliminates collisions on the switch and dedicates all port bandwidth to the connected host. CSMA/CD is a method for detecting Ethernet collisions on older hubs and bridges. It is no longer required with full-duplex switch ports. Each frame is assigned a random time to re-send a frame when collisions occur.

Switching Methods

Cut-Through Switching

The cut-through switching technique optimizes performance by examining only the first six bytes (destination MAC address) of an Ethernet frame before making a forwarding decision. The switch does a MAC address table lookup for the destination MAC address and forwards the frame. The advantage is the forwarding decision is made before all of the frame arrives and thereby minimizing network latency.

Store-and-Forward Switching

The store-and-forward method is traditional switching where the frame is not forwarded until all of the frame has arrived. The switch copies the frame to memory before examining the destination MAC address and forwarding the frame.

Cisco Express Forwarding (CEF)

CEF is a layer 3 switching technique that creates FIB and adjacency tables for optimized packet forwarding. It is only available on routers and switch platforms with routing enabled and the required hardware.

MAC Learning and Aging

MAC address learning occurs when the switch is first started and connected hosts start sending frames. In addition MAC learning is triggered when the aging time expires. The switch removes MAC address table entries every five minutes as a default.

The layer 2 broadcast is forwarded to all devices on a single broadcast (segment) domain. The switch creates the broadcast packet **ffff.ffff.ffff** as the destination MAC address and forwards it out all ports except where the frame was learned. The port where the frame was learned is the sending host. Note that broadcast frames are created and never learned from an inbound switch port.

The following summarizes what happens when a host sends a packet to a server on the same VLAN for the first time.

1. The switch adds the source MAC address of the incoming frame if it is not listed in the MAC address table.

2. The switch does a MAC address table lookup for the destination MAC address.

3. The switch floods the frame using destination MAC address **ffff.ffff.ffff** out all ports except the port where the source MAC address was learned.

4. The server with the assigned MAC address responds with a frame that lists the MAC address.

34

5. The switch updates the MAC address table with the MAC address of the server. That is the destination MAC address for frames sent from the host.

6. The switch forwards the frames from the host to the server based on the switch port assigned to the server.

Unicast MAC Flooding

The switch will first flood the local VLAN segment (unicast MAC flooding) to determine if the host is local. The ARP broadcast is only sent for packet forwarding between local and remote hosts on different VLANs or subnets. Unknown unicast frames are retransmitted only to ports that belong to the same VLAN

Broadcast Domain

The VLAN creates a broadcast domain that is defined by assigning switch port/s to the same VLAN. All hosts connected to switch ports of the same VLAN are part of the same broadcast domain. Creating multiple VLANs defines multiple broadcast domains. Switches do not forward broadcast or multicast traffic between VLANs minimizing bandwidth utilization compared with hubs and bridges. The switch only forwards unicasts, broadcasts and multicasts on the same segment (VLAN).

Frame Switching

The host sends packets with an IP header encapsulated in a frame. The source and destination IP address in the header are required for end-to-end connectivity. Layer 2 switches do not examine or understand IP addressing.

Switches and wireless access points are network devices that make forwarding decisions based on the destination MAC address in the frame. They do not change MAC addressing in the frame. Wireless access points are essentially bridges.

The switch does not rewrite MAC addressing in the frame header. It examines the source MAC address and destination MAC address. The source MAC address of the incoming frame is added to the MAC address table if it isn't listed.

The switch examines the frame header for the destination MAC address and does a MAC address table lookup to make a forwarding decision. The frame is then forwarded out the switch port associated with the destination MAC address where the host is connected. Any destination MAC address that is not local is forwarded to the router. The IP addressing does not change between source and destination.

- switches use the MAC address in a frame to make forwarding decisions
- switches forward frames and don't rewrite source or destination MAC address

Routers make forwarding decisions based on source and destination IP address. The router will do a routing table lookup then rewrite the source and destination MAC address in the frame header.

Frame Switching Examples

Example 1:

Refer to the network drawing where Host-1 has sent a packet to Server-1. The destination MAC address is unknown. The switch will unicast flood (learning) the frame out all ports except the port where the frame was learned from (Gi1/1). Server-1 with the matching destination MAC address receives the frame and sends a frame to Switch-1. The switch updates the MAC address table with the MAC address and associated port (Gi1/3) of Server-1.

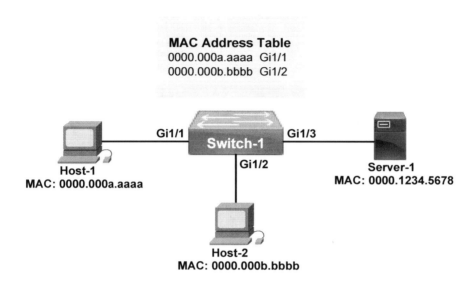

MAC Address Table
0000.000a.aaaa Gi1/1
0000.000b.bbbb Gi1/2

Gi1/1 — Switch-1 — Gi1/3

Gi1/2

Host-1
MAC: 0000.000a.aaaa

Server-1
MAC: 0000.1234.5678

Host-2
MAC: 0000.000b.bbbb

Example 2:

Refer to the network drawing where Host-2 has sent a packet to Server-1. The switch will examine the source and destination MAC address of the frame arriving on port Gi1/2 from Host-2. The MAC address table has no entry for either MAC address. The switch will then add the source MAC address (Host-2) to the MAC table. In addition the switch will unicast flood (MAC learning) the frame out all ports except the port where the frame was learned from (Gi1/2). Server-1 with the matching destination MAC address receives the frame and sends a frame to the switch. The switch updates the MAC address table with the MAC address of Server-1.

- 0000.000b.bbbb will be added to the MAC address table
- frame will be forwarded out all active switch ports except port Gi1/2

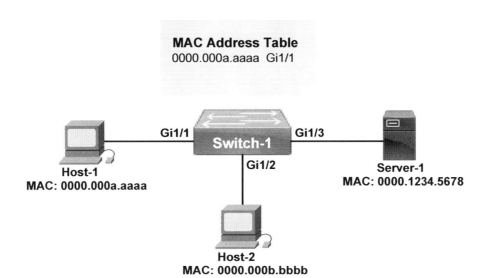

MAC Address Table
0000.000a.aaaa Gi1/1

Example 3:

Refer to the network drawing where Host-2 has sent a packet to Server-1. Switch-1 will examine the incoming frame from Host-2 arriving on port Gi1/2. The switch will do a MAC table lookup based on the destination MAC address. The switch determines the destination MAC address is assigned to Server-1. The frame is forwarded to port Gi1/3 associated with Server-1.

- switch will examine the frame and do a MAC address table lookup
- frame is forwarded out switch port Gi1/3

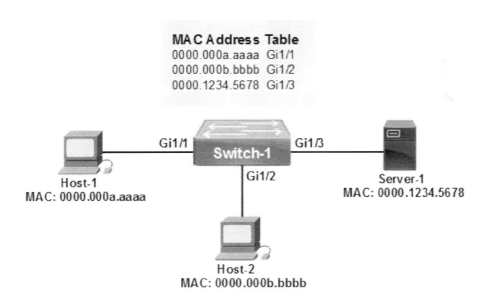

MAC Address Table
0000.000a.aaaa Gi1/1
0000.000b.bbbb Gi1/2
0000.1234.5678 Gi1/3

2.2 Interpret Ethernet Frame Format

The Cyclic Redundancy Check (CRC) is a number (FCS) calculated on each frame received to verify data integrity. The layer 2 frame is discarded if the received FCS number doesn't match the original. It is an error detection technique and not error recovery. Any error detection and/or error recovery is managed by transport layer 4 protocols. The source MAC address (SA) and destination MAC address (DA) are 6 bytes. The following are the fields that comprise an Ethernet frame.

- FCS
- type/length
- preamble
- source MAC address (6 bytes)
- destination MAC address (6 bytes)
- payload (variable)

2.3 Troubleshoot Interface and Cabling Errors

Show Interfaces

The results provided by the **show interfaces** command include layer 1 and layer 2 status information for all or individual network interfaces (ethernet, serial etc).

> Interface = Layer 1, Line protocol = Layer 2

The possible interface states for interface and line protocol include **up, down** or **administratively down**. The normal status of an Ethernet interface is up/up. The **shutdown** command would change interface status to admin down. (i.e **down/down**) It is not possible to have line protocol in **up** state when the interface is **down** (down/up).

The following commands verify interface and line protocol status for a switch interface:

- switch# **show interfaces**
- switch# **show protocols**

switch# **show interfaces fastethernet1/1**

> *FastEthernet 1/1 **up**, line protocol **up** (normal state)*

Typical Interface Errors:

Layer 1 = cabling, switch configuration mismatches (speed/duplex) errors.

Layer 2 = encapsulation mismatch, spanning tree, clocking errors.

This example has the interface (layer 1) *up* and line protocol (layer 2) *down*. The Ethernet signaling is working and there are no issues with cabling. The problem is at the data link layer or higher. It is possible as well that layer 3 routing or IP addressing issues are causing the error however that is unknown.

switch# **show interfaces fastethernet0/1**

FastEthernet 0/1 ***up****, line protocol* ***down***

The **show interfaces** command provide the following operational status and configuration settings.

switch# **show interfaces**

- interface status
- interface errors
- encapsulation
- MAC address
- IP address
- subnet mask
- MTU size

Duplex Setting

The Gigabit Ethernet switch port supports full-duplex traffic between the host and network switch. That eliminates collisions and creates a collision domain per port. The fact that there are no collisions increase throughput and decreases network latency. Hosts connected to a full-duplex switch port create a collision domain per port.

Traffic can be sent simultaneously in both directions between the host and network switch. That effectively doubles the bandwidth available from 1 Gbps to 2 Gbps. The default setting for Ethernet Gigabit and higher is full-duplex mode.

Gigabit Ethernet switch ports have eliminated collisions unless there is a configuration error or hardware issue. Collisions are caused most often when there is a duplex mismatches on connected interfaces. In addition collisions can occur when there is a bad network interface card (NIC) or cabling error. The switch increments collision counter error after sending 512 bits of a frame.

The following are preferred duplex settings to minimize interface errors on switch links:

- configure full-duplex setting on both switch link interfaces
- configure auto-negotiation on both switch link interfaces

Duplex mismatches with a neighbor interface can cause the following interface errors:

- collisions
- input errors
- CRC errors
- slow performance

The cause of collisions on a broadcast domain (VLAN) instead of interfaces are typically the result of duplex mismatches and faulty network interface card (NIC).

Ethernet Interface MTU

MTU refers to the maximum size (bytes) of an Ethernet frame. The default Ethernet MTU is 1500 bytes. The frame is comprised of a header and payload (data). The header is a fixed size with fields for control and MAC addressing. Decreasing the MTU size would decrease the payload amount (bytes) that can be transmitted.

- default = 1500 bytes

- jumbo = 9216 bytes

- baby giant = 1600 bytes

- runt = < 64 bytes

The output of **show interfaces** is used for troubleshooting various Layer 1 and layer 2 interface errors. Layer 2 errors include runts, giants, collisions and CRC errors. The most common cause of CRC and runts is collisions. Giant frames result from either a bad NIC card or an MTU configuration error

Ethernet interfaces that are in err-disabled state cannot send or receive frames and are essentially shutdown. It is a layer 2 error and the cause is operational or a configuration mismatch. The following are some typical causes of err-disabled state:

- duplex mismatch
- port security violation
- EtherChannel mode mismatch
- UDLD errors

Troubleshooting Example:

Refer to the network drawing. There are a high number of input errors and CRC errors on Switch-2. That indicates there is a layer 1 issue between the switches. Switch-1 is sending frames that are corrupt when they arrive at Switch-2. The most probable cause is duplex mismatch between the switch interfaces or cabling errors.

The switch ports must agree on the duplex setting. Gigabit Ethernet ports do not use half-duplex at all. The Cisco switch default setting is **duplex auto** (for full-duplex mode. There is however the option to hard code with the interface command **duplex full**. The speed setting must match between switches as well. That is configured with the **speed auto** command or hard code with **speed 1000**. Since the frames were arriving at Switch-2, verify the duplex setting on Switch-1 to start with. Cabling defects require replacement when the correct cable type is currently used to fix layer 1 issues

2.4 <u>Configure, Verify and Troubleshoot Normal/Extended Range VLANs</u>

The primary purpose of a VLAN is to create a broadcast domain defined by assigning a single or multiple switch ports. All unicast, broadcast and multicast traffic is limited to the VLAN. That conserves bandwidth usage across the switching infrastructure.

The following are the guidelines for deploying VLANs to a Cisco switch.

- Normal Range VLANs = 1 - 1005
- Extended Range VLANs = 1006 - 4094
- VLAN 1, 1002 - 1005 are automatically created and cannot be deleted
- VLAN 1006 - 4094 cannot be pruned from a trunk

All switch ports are assigned to VLAN 1 as a default configuration for Cisco switches. In addition VLAN 1 is used for management traffic and cannot be deleted. The normal range VLANs (2-1001) can be added, modified and deleted from the switch. Cisco recommends assigning all data and voice traffic to a non-default VLAN.

Advantages of VLANs

VLANs do not prevent broadcast storms, they minimize the size and effect of the broadcast storm on neighbor switches and hosts. The VLAN is a broadcast domain and as such broadcasts are not advertised outside of the VLAN minimizing bandwidth usage and multicast traffic.

1. Enable access to network services based on logical requirements such as company organization and department.

2. Network security is optimized with VLANs by segmenting sensitive traffic and segmenting it from other network traffic.

3. Bandwidth efficiency is accomplished through segmenting traffic into smaller broadcast domains. Unicasts, broadcasts and multicasts are not forwarded between VLANs minimizing bandwidth utilization.

4. Ease add/move/delete administration of hosts on the network and scalability for larger enterprise deployments.

Access Ports (data and voice)

The switch access port provides connectivity for access devices such as a desktops, servers and wireless access points. The switch port can only be assigned one VLAN unless you are connecting an IP phone. The data VLAN and voice VLAN is permitted on an access port with the following configuration commands.

switch(config)# **interface fastethernet0/1**
switch(config-if)# **switchport mode access** *(configure access port mode for Fa0/1)*
switch(config-if)# **switchport access vlan 9** *(assign vlan 9 to data traffic)*
switch(config-if)# **switchport voice vlan 10** *(assign vlan 10 to voice traffic)*

The following commands list all VLANs configured on a switch. That includes VLAN number, VLAN name, status and port assigned.

switch# **show vlan**
switch# **show vlan brief**

The following command is used to verify any/all switch ports assigned to a single VLAN.

switch# **show vlan id** [vlan]

The Cisco switch port supports access mode or trunk mode. The network administrator configures the port mode when enabling the interface. The standard layer 2 switch port is referred to as an access port. Switch access ports that receives a packet with an 802.1q tag in the header will discard the packet without learning source MAC address.

Interface Range

The following IOS command creates and assigns VLAN 10 to switch port range Gi1/1 through Gi1/24 interfaces. There is no requirement to first create the VLAN in global configuration mode. The vlan.dat file is the VLAN database where the switch VLAN configuration is stored.

switch(config)# **interface range gigabitethernet1/1-24**
switch(config-if)# **switchport mode access**
switch(config-if)# **switchport access vlan 10**

Switchport Command

The ***administrative mode*** is the switch port configuration and ***operational mode*** is the interface status. The switch won't setup a trunk unless the switch port mode on both switch ports are configured to trunk VLANs.

Administrative Mode

- trunk
- dynamic desirable
- dynamic auto
- static access

Operational Mode

- trunk
- static access
- down

Default VLAN

VLAN 1 is the default for any Cisco switch that has no initial configuration. The primary purpose of VLAN 1 is to forward management traffic between switches. The following statements correctly describe VLAN 1:

- All switch ports are assigned to VLAN 1 as a default.
- Default VLAN 1 forwards management traffic and cannot be deleted.
- Assigning data and/or voice traffic to VLAN 1 creates a security vulnerability.

Default Gateway

The **ip default-gateway** command on a switch configures the IP address of the router interface to forward packets when the destination is on a different VLAN or subnet.

The following IOS command will configure a connected upstream router as the default gateway for the switch. The router has an interface with IP address 172.16.1.254 on interface Gi0/1. The switch forwards packets to the default gateway for layer 3 services. That could include ARP requests, Inter-VLAN routing and remote subnet connectivity.

> switch-1(config)# **ip default-gateway 172.16.1.254**

Refer to the network drawing. The default gateway is the upstream layer 3 device (router) that provides routing services. The default gateway for Host-1 is 172.16.1.254. The IP address of the directly connected interface (Gi0/0) to the layer 2 switch is assigned as default gateway for the host. The host, switch and default gateway must be in the same subnet.

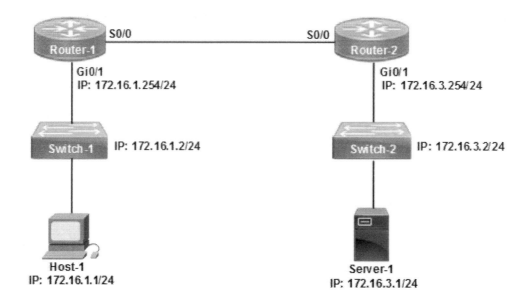

Default Cisco switch configuration

- single broadcast domain (VLAN 1)
- all hosts are in the same broadcast domain
- switch port mode is unassigned
- switch with lowest MAC address is the root bridge
- VTY lines are not enabled

2.5 Configure, Verify and Troubleshoot Inter-Switch Connectivity

Trunk Ports

The purpose of a switch trunk is to forward multiple VLANs between switches. The switch port must be configured for trunk mode to enable forwarding of multiple VLANs. That allows communication between hosts assigned to the same VLAN that spans switches. Forwarding multiple VLANs across a switch link requires trunk mode to enable the VLAN tagging feature.

switch(config-if)# **switchport mode trunk**

The following show commands display configuration information for all trunk interfaces.

switch# **show interfaces trunk**
switch# **show interface switchport**

The IOS commands display the following trunk operational and configuration settings:

- tunk operational status
- switch port members
- VLANs allowed
- native VLAN
- encapsulation type
- trunk mode

Configuring a switch port as a trunk requires enabling trunk mode and 802.1q encapsulation. The following trunk is static and DTP trunk negotiation is not used.

    switch(config)# **interface fastethernet0/1**
    switch(config-if)# **switchport mode trunk**
    switch(config-if)# **encapsulation dot1q**
    switch(config-if)# **end**

Native VLAN

The native VLAN is used to forward control traffic across the switch trunk. Changing the native VLAN from VLAN 1 to any available nondefault VLAN is a Cisco security best practice. There are security vulnerabilities associated with the default VLAN 1. In addition STP issues are minimized by selecting a nondefault VLAN instead of VLAN 1.

Control traffic (CDP, PAgP, VTP, STP and DTP) always uses VLAN 1 and travel on the native VLAN (untagged traffic) by *default*. The trunk tags all data VLANs for identification purposes. The untagged traffic is separated from data traffic as a result.

None of the control traffic except STP and DTP are forwarded across the native VLAN when the native VLAN is changed to a nondefault value. STP and DTP are management protocols that must be untagged across trunk links.

The following command changes the native VLAN from default VLAN 1 to VLAN 999.

    switch(config-if)# **switchport trunk native vlan 999**

The native VLAN configured on a trunk link must match between switches to forward untagged packets across the trunk correctly. VLAN hopping is a security vulnerability caused by native VLAN mismatch. STP and DTP can detect native VLAN mismatches.

VLAN Pruning

The purpose of VLAN pruning is to permit or deny VLANs across a switch trunk. The Cisco default is to allow all VLANs across the trunk. The switch is configured for VLAN pruning won't forward specific VLANs across a switch trunk. The local switch alerts the neighbor switch of all local VLANs that are not active (not configured).

Any VLANs that are not configured are pruned by the neighbor switch to minimize unicast, broadcast and multicast traffic across the trunk. The Cisco default trunk configuration allows all VLANs from the range 1 - 4094 across the trunk.

The following IOS command will *only allow* VLAN 10, VLAN 11 and VLAN 12 across the trunk. The network administrator can add or remove VLANs after that IOS command is issued based on requirements. The command permits commas for multiple non-consecutive VLANs or hyphen to specify a range of consecutive VLANs.

> switch(config-if)# **switchport trunk allowed vlan 10-12**

The **add | remove** keyword only applies after pruning has already occurred on the trunk interface to limit the VLANs allowed from the default range (1-4094). Configure the following IOS command to allow only a single VLAN or multiple VLANs. Cisco switches permit assigning a range of VLANs as well.

> switch(config-if)# **switchport trunk allowed vlan add** [vlan id, vlan id, ...]

The following IOS command will remove VLAN 10 from the trunk. That will filter all traffic from that VLAN so it cannot traverse the trunk link between switches. To remove a range of consecutive VLANs such as from VLAN 1 to VLAN 100 inclusive, use a hyphen (1-100). For a non-consecutive list such as VLAN 1 and VLAN 10,11,12 use commas and hyphens (1,10-12).

> switch(config-if)# **switchport trunk allowed vlan remove 10**

The following IOS interface command will add VLAN 12 to the trunk interface. That will permit all traffic from that VLAN so it can traverse the trunk link between switches. To add a range of consecutive VLANs such as from VLAN 1 to VLAN 100 inclusive, use a hyphen (1-100). For the example where there is a non-consecutive list such as VLAN 1 and VLAN 10,11,12 use commas and hyphens (1,10-12).

> switch(config-if)# **switchport trunk allowed vlan add 12**

Dynamic Trunking Protocol (DTP)

The switch port is configured as a trunk to enable trunking. The trunk is setup with a neighbor switch using static or dynamic negotiation. The static trunk is a manual configuration that isn't based on any negotiation protocol.

- DTP enables dynamic negotiation of a trunk between two switches.
- DTP modes are *nonegotiate*, *desirable* and *auto*.
- DTP is enabled by default

The DTP request frames are sent to the neighbor switch to negotiate the trunk setup. Cisco switches use the default **auto** mode. The switch port configured with *desirable* or *auto* mode listen for DTP requests. In addition the switch port configured with *desirable* mode actively sends DTP frames to establish trunk with neighbor.

The switches on both sides of the link are configured with the command *switchport mode trunk*. It is equivalent to the *on* keyword for dynamic trunking. DTP provides dynamic negotiation based on the *switchport mode dynamic auto* or *switchport mode dynamic desirable* commands.

The following describe the effect of each static and DTP mode:

switchport mode access = no trunking
switchport mode trunk = static (on) mode

switchport mode dynamic auto = listens for DTP requests
switchport mode dynamic desirable = listens/sends DTP requests
switchport mode nonegotiate = disable DTP

The following describes how each switch mode affects trunk setup between local and remote switches. Access mode is equivalent to a switch access port (no trunk). The **on** mode is configured manually at the switch (static trunk) and not a DTP mode.

Table 2-1 Dynamic Trunking Protocol Modes

local switch	neighbor switch	result
auto	auto	access port
auto	desirable	trunk
auto	on	trunk
desirable	on	trunk
desirable	desirable	trunk
nonegotiate	nonegotiate	access port
nonegotiate	on	trunk

When two connected ports are connected and at least one of the ports is configured as *desirable*, the two switches will negotiate the formation of a trunk across the link.

DTP *auto* mode supports access mode and trunk mode. The neighbor incoming negotiation would determine whether the switch port operational mode is trunk or static access. DTP *auto* allows the port to negotiate DTP if the other side is set to trunk or desirable. The *nonegotiate* mode is configured on both switch interfaces that do not support DTP mode or should not establish trunking.

The following are methods for disabling DTP on a switch link:

- switchport nonegotiate
- switchport mode access
- static trunk

Troubleshooting

The following are common causes of trunking errors:

- VLAN mismatches
- incorrect trunk mode
- VLANs not allowed (pruned)

VLAN Trunking Protocol (VTP)

- VTP enable VLAN configuration automatically across multiple switches
- VTP enables synchronization of VLANs between subnets

VTP Requirements

- configure all switch uplink ports to trunk
- designate at least one VTP server
- configure all switches with the same VTP domain name and password
- switch must be in VTP server or transparent mode before configuring VLANs

The primary feature enhancements available with VTP v2 include the following:

- Token Ring VLANs
- VLAN consistency check
- transparent mode switch forwards VTP advertisements with no version check

The VTP modes assignable to a Cisco switch are client, server and transparent. The default mode is server when enabling VTP.

802.1q Encapsulation

Trunking enables forwarding of multiple VLANs across a single switch link. Ports between switches must be configured with trunk mode to forward multiple VLANs across a switch link. The 802.1q protocol is an encapsulation method that enables forwarding of multiple VLANs across the switch link. The 802.1q tag has a 12 bit VLAN ID field used for identifying VLAN membership of the frame. The switch adds an 802.1q tag to each Ethernet frame with VLAN membership. That allows the switches to identify the VLAN for each arriving frame. The Ethernet frame header is modified as a result of adding the VLAN tag. That requires recalculation of the FCS value used for CRC.

The following are the primary characteristics of 802.1q encapsulation.

- open standard for multi-vendor switch connectivity
- default setting for Cisco switches
- provides VLAN tagging across a switch trunk

2.6 <u>Configure, Verify and Troubleshoot STP Protocols</u>

The primary reason for deploying Spanning Tree is to prevent layer 2 loops and broadcast storms where frames are forwarded in a loop between switches. The most current STP protocol supports per VLAN instances (PVST+).

Redundant topologies are characterized by multiple paths that could cause layer 2 loops. STP is deployed to forward and block specific ports to eliminate forwarding loops between switches. Specific problems caused by redundant topology include sending multiple frames, broadcast storms and MAC address table instability. Some possible problems that can occur when configuring redundant links between switches:

- additional frames sent
- broadcast storms
- MAC address table instability

STP creates a loop free layer 2 topology by configuring some switch ports to forward traffic and some to block traffic. That is based on electing a root bridge. The switch with the lowest bridge ID is elected root bridge. The bridge ID is comprised of priority setting and MAC address. STP calculates lowest path cost for each neighbor interface to the root bridge. The neighbor switch port that receives the best BPDU (least cost to the root bridge) is assigned root port for that switch.

The BPDU is a Spanning Tree Protocol message that is sent between switches. The hello timer setting is the interval between BPDU advertisements. The BPDU messages contains STP information from the sending switch. That includes STP timers, root bridge ID, sender bridge ID and port (path) cost.

STP will assign a port type to each switch port uplink and an STP interface state for each port as well. The purpose is to create a loop free layer 2 topology. The switching infrastructure is Layer 2 converged when spanning tree has elected a root bridge, designated ports, root ports, backup ports and alternate ports. In addition RSTP switch ports are forwarding or discarding. Frames are forwarded after trunk is established (where applicable) and STP election has occurred.

There are four STP port states with the original 802.1d STP:

- blocking
- listening
- learning = populating MAC address table
- forwarding

STP Mode (PVST+ and RPVST+)

Per VLAN Spanning Tree Plus (PVST+) enables a separate 802.1d spanning tree instance per VLAN. It was developed to support 802.1q encapsulation for Cisco devices only. The original 802.1d standard was designed for a single broadcast domain. VLAN based spanning tree for any switching topology permits only one root bridge per VLAN.

Per VLAN Spanning Tree (PVST) assigns one root bridge per VLAN. Spanning Tree Protocol elects only one root port to a switch where there are redundant links. The root port transitions to forwarding state and sends frames to the root bridge. There is a root port elected for every neighbor that connects to the root bridge (switch). All switch uplinks for the root bridge are designated ports and transitioned to forwarding state. The default VLAN bridge priority value for a Cisco switch is 32768. The switch with the lowest MAC address is elected as the root bridge when priority values are equal. The interface port priority setting can change the preferred forwarding interface on a switch.

The newer 802.1w (RSTP) standard is comprised of three port states. They include *discarding, learning and forwarding*. The discarding state is new to RPVST and equivalent to the blocking and listening states of older 802.1d protocol. The single RSTP discarding state enables faster convergence

Verify PVST+

Refer to the exhibit. The IOS command **show spanning-tree vlan 10** provides per VLAN spanning tree status for VLAN 10. The **rstp** indicates 802.1w is enabled and Switch-1 is assigned as the root bridge for VLAN 10. The root bridge priority (**28682**) is lower than the default 32768. Root bridge ports are always designated ports and in forwarding state.

```
switch-1# show spanning-tree vlan 10

VLAN 0010
Spanning tree enabled protocol rstp
Root ID Priority 28682
Address: 0000.abcd.aaaa
This bridge is the root
Hello Time 2 sec   Max Age 20 sec   Forward Delay 15 sec
Bridge ID priority 28682
Address 0000.abcd.aaaa
Hello Time 2 sec   Max Age 20 sec   Forward Delay 15 sec
Aging Time 300

Interface  Role   Sts   Cost   Prio.Nbr   Type
---------- ------ ----- ------ ---------- -------
Gi1/1      Desg   FWD   4      128.1      P2p
Gi1/1      Desg   FWD   4      128.1      P2p
Gi1/1      Desg   FWD   4      128.1      P2p
```

- rstp = state of discarding, learning or forwarding
- root bridge priority is lower than the default value for spanning tree.
- all root bridge ports are designated ports are in a forwarding state.
- local switch is the root bridge for VLAN 10

The following IOS global configuration command enables RSTP on a switch.

switch(config)# **spanning-tree mode rapid-pvst**

The advantage of Rapid Spanning Tree Protocol (RSTP) is faster layer 2 convergence than the older 802.1 standard. The newer standard is 802.1w and includes the following features to minimize convergence time.

- BPDUs are now advertised from all switches instead of from the root bridge only.

- The amount of time is decreased to three hello packets (BPDUs) before detecting root switch link failure.

- Three port states: discarding, learning and forwarding for faster convergence.

- RSTP convergence includes forwarding and discarding states.

- There are two additional STP port types: alternate and backup.

- RSTP is compatible with the original IEEE 802.1d STP

Alternate Port

Replaces the 802.1d blocking state. The alternate port as with all RSTP ports are actively forwarding or discarding. The discarding is equivalent to the older listening state. It transitions from discarding to forwarding immediately when the designated port fails so there is no waiting for convergence.

Backup Port

Requires a hub with two switch links (single collision domain) to provide additional redundancy for faster convergence to the access layer. The RSTP proposal/agreement process is based on a handshake between point-to-point neighbor switch links. It provides current root bridge state information to all switches. It is not a timer-based proposal/agreement as with the original 802.1d (STP).

STP Root Bridge Selection

The default priority of a Cisco switch is 32768. STP selects the root bridge (switch) with the lowest priority. The switch with the lowest bridge ID is elected when all switches have the same priority. The bridge ID is calculated from the priority setting and MAC address. The switch with the lowest MAC address becomes the root bridge as a result.

The Spanning Tree election assigns root bridge along with designated ports, root ports and alternate ports to neighbor switches. The root port is a switch port on a neighbor switch that has the least cost path to the root bridge. It is a primary forwarding link to the root bridge.

Example 1:

Refer to the network drawing. The root bridge switch ports are all assigned as designated ports by STP. The switch with the lowest bridge ID is assigned as root bridge. The switch priorities are all equal (32768) so the switch with the lowest MAC address is elected root bridge. The designated ports of a root bridge connect to the root port of non-root bridge (switch) neighbors. The root port of a non-root bridge is the switch port with the lowest cost to the root bridge. That is a directly connected switch port with the highest bandwidth. That creates the primary links for switch traffic.

The lowest MAC address is calculated from left to right per hexidecimal number. All numbers match until number 9 where Switch-3 has the lower (a) compared with Switch-2 (b) and Switch-1 (c). As a result, Switch-3 is elected as root bridge. In addition all switch ports on a root bridge are all designated ports.

> Switch-1 = 0000.abcd.cccc
> Switch-2 = 0000.abcd.bbbb
> Switch-3 = 0000.abcd.**aaaa** = **root bridge**

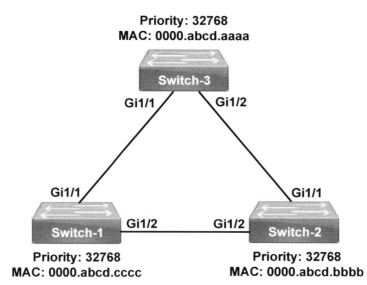

The non-root switches are assigned a designated port as well to forward BPDUs on the network segment. The designated port connects to a neighbor non-root bridge. The non-root switches compare link cost (bandwidth) for that switch link (network segment). The switch port with the lower cost (highest bandwidth) is the designated port for that link. When the switch ports are equal-cost, the port of the non-root switch with the lower bridge ID is assigned as a designated port.

The two non-root switches are Switch-1 and Switch-2. There is a single Gigabit Ethernet link connecting the non-root switches. As a result the switch port cost to the network segment is equal. The port of the non-root switch with the lower bridge ID is assigned as a designated port when path costs are equal. Switch-2 has a lower bridge-ID than Switch-1. As a result Switch-2 port Gi1/2 is a designated port as well. Switch-1 port Gi1/2 is blocking/alternate port type to prevent layer 2 loops.

Switch-1
- Gi1/1 = Root Port
- Gi1/2 = Blocking/Alternate Port

Switch-2
- Gi1/1 = Root Port
- Gi1/2 = Designated Port

Switch-3
- Gi1/1 = Designated Port
- Gi1/2 = Designated Port

Example 2:

The bridge ID is a numerical value for a switch based on the priority setting and MAC address. The bridge ID is calculated by STP to assign the root bridge for a VLAN. The switch with the lowest bridge ID is elected as root bridge. The lowest MAC address becomes the tie breaker when none of the switches have the lowest priority.

The example has two switches (option C and option D) with the same lowest priority of 28673. The tie breaker is the switch with the lower MAC address. Counting from right to left, the **1** of option D is lower than **A** of option C. Hexidecimal **A** is equivalent to the number 10. The switch from option D is elected as root bridge.

28673: 0000.000**a**.aaaa
28673: 0000.000**1**.2345

2.7 Configure, Verify and Troubleshoot STP Enhancements

PortFast

Spanning Tree Protocol (STP) enhancements are designed to optimize network convergence. The uplink interfaces that connect switches are part of STP election. The switching topology is often complex with multiple redundant links. The access layer connects hosts on single point-to-point links where Layer 2 loops do not occur.

PortFast is enabled on access switch ports where hosts and wireless access points are connected. That allows the switch ports to transition from disabled or blocking state to *forwarding* state immediately on startup. The following IOS command enables PortFast on a switch access port.

> switch(config-if)# **spanning-tree portfast**

BPDU guard

The purpose of BPDU guard is to err-disable (shutdown) an access switch port when BPDUs are received from a network device. BPDU guard is enabled on an access switch port or globally where hosts and supported devices connect. BPDU guard is configured on switch interface to prevent network devices from affecting the STP topology. For instance connecting a new switch to your cubicle jack triggers an STP recalculation. The new switch is now connected to an access switch port causing a layer 2 topology change notification. The consequences could include a new root bridge election. The following command enables BPDU guard on a switch access port.

> switch(config-if)# **spanning-tree bpduguard enable**

2.8 Configure and Verify Layer 2 Protocols

Cisco Discovery Protocol (CDP)

CDP is a Layer 2 Cisco proprietary neighbor discovery protocol. The purpose is to discover operational and configuration information for directly connected Cisco devices. The purpose of CDP is to detect and relay device information to neighbor devices.

In addition Cisco CDP can only detect Cisco devices including IP phones. The Cisco IP phone appears to CDP as a unique neighbor device with an IP address. During bootup, the IP phone receives voice VLAN configuration from the access switch.

Configure CDP

CDP is enabled on Cisco devices globally by default including network interfaces. The following command re-enables CDP globally after it has been disabled.

> switch(config)# **cdp run**

54

The following interface level command re-enables CDP on a specific network interface after it has been disabled.

> switch(config-if)# **cdp enable**

There is additional neighbor configuration information available with the **detail** keyword used with **show cdp neighbor** IOS command. The detail keyword includes IOS version of connected neighbors.

> switch# **show cdp neighbor detail**

- CDP is enabled by default both globally and on all network interfaces.
- The default CDP update timer = 60 seconds.

Link Layer Discovery Protocol (LLDP)

LLDP is the open standard counterpart to Cisco CDP for network discovery in a multi-vendor environment. Cisco supports LLDP (IEEE 802.1ab) and thereby optimizing auto-discovery and network management. The network devices share identity and feature support functionality via LLDP and with neighbors.

- The default packet update interval for LLDP is 30 seconds.

- LLDP is an open standard network discovery protocol specified with IEEE 802.1ab standard.

- Cisco IP phones are enabled for LLDP when LLDP packets are first sent from the phone to the switch.

The following global configuration command enables LLDP globally on a Cisco switch.

> switch(config)# **lldp run**

The following IOS interface level command enables a Cisco switch to receive LLDP packets on an interface.

> switch(config-if)# **lldp receive**

Verify LLDP

Table 2-2 Show Commands to Verify LLDP Status

show lldp	verify LLDP is enabled and global timers
show lldp neighbors detail	list Ethernet media, interface description
show lldp interface	list the LLDP interfaces enabled

2.9 <u>Configure, Verify and Troubleshoot EtherChannel</u>

EtherChannel bundles multiple physical switch links between switches into a single logical link. It is sometimes referred to as switch port aggregation. The advantages include fault tolerance (redundancy) and high speed connectivity between switches. Cisco switches support assigning a maximum 8 ports to a single Etherchannel bundle. LACP supports a maximum 16 ports however only 8 can be active simultaneously. The additional ports are used for failover purposes.

Traffic from a previously single Gigabit Ethernet port can now forward traffic across a logical link at higher speed. For instance bundling four separate Gigabit Ethernet links into a single EtherChannel creates a 4 Gbps link. In addition all traffic is forwarded across all available links when any single link isn't available.

The options for configuring EtherChannel include static or dynamic protocols:

1. Static does not provide any dynamic trunk negotiation. The channel-group is configured with **on** keyword for all switches ports on both switches assigned to the EtherChannel.

2. PAgP is a Cisco proprietary protocol that provides dynamic negotiation of an EtherChannel link. It supports Cisco network devices only and configured with the **channel-group** command. The four PAgP modes include ***on, off, auto*** and ***desirable.***

3. LACP is an open standard that supports EtherChannel between different switch vendors. It supports negotiating of dynamic EtherChannel links as well. The four modes supported include ***on***, ***off, active and passive.***

Port Channel

There are Layer 2 and Layer 3 port channel interfaces. The **channel-group** number binds the port channel interface to an Etherchannel. The Layer 2 port channel is a logical interface comprised of Etherchannel access ports or trunk ports. The Layer 2 port channel is created automatically based on the **channel-group** number. The supported channel-group numbers are 1 - 4096. The Layer 3 port channel is a routed logical interface comprised of EtherChannel access ports or trunk ports. The following is an example of a Layer 3 port channel

> switch(config)# **interface port-channel 1**
> switch(config-if)# **no switchport**
> switch(config-if)# **ip address 172.16.1.1 255.255.255.0**

The following show command lists the port channel and line protocol interface status (up/up). In addition the port channel members are listed along with interface errors.

> switch# **show interface port-channel** [number]

56

Troubleshooting EtherChannel

The following settings must match on EtherChannel switch ports that connect switches. The port state is err-disabled when the Etherchannel interface is misconfigured.

- duplex
- speed
- protocol mode
- switchport mode
- VLAN
- STP
- native VLAN

Example:

Host-1 from VLAN 10 cannot communicate with Server-1 assigned to VLAN 10.

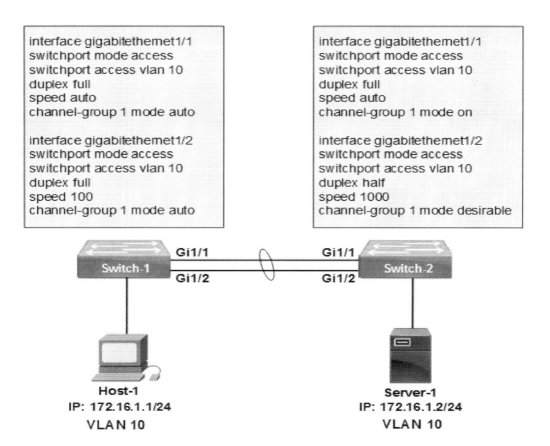

The network topology drawing is an EtherChannel between two switches connecting Host-1 to Server-1. In addition Host-1 and Server-1 are on the same subnet and same VLAN. It is a layer 2 configuration similar to any data center design. The access ports are forwarding single VLAN (no trunk required).

1. All switch ports assigned to an EtherChannel must be configured with matching settings to prevent err-disable state. The speed, duplex, switchport mode, STP, VLAN membership and protocol mode (PAgP/LACP) must match for each port.

2. Switch-1 (Gi1/1) to Switch-2 (Gi1/1) have a PAgP mode mismatch between switch ports. EtherChannel requires desirable mode on at least one switch port to enable it.

3. Switch-1 (Gi1/2) to Switch-2 (Gi1/2) have a duplex and speed mismatch between switch ports. The correct settings for Gigabit speed or higher is 1000 or auto. The supported duplex setting is half, full or auto however full-duplex is the Cisco default.

EtherChannel across a trunk link requires the native VLAN, allowed VLANs and encapsulation type to match as well.

2.10 <u>Describe the Benefits of Switch Stacking and Chassis Aggregation</u>

Switch Stacking creates a single logical switch from up to nine Catalyst switches where supported. The advantages include easier management of a single switch instead of of multiple switches. In addition there is faster network convergence with fewer switch uplinks to neighbors.

The Stack elects a stack master switch and a standby master switch. There is 1:N (multiple switch failover) redundancy per stack. Every switch is eligible for election as master or standby. The Stacking cable provides redundant data paths between stack neighbors. Link redundancy is enabled with Cross-stack EtherChannel between stacks.

3.0 Routing Technologies

3.1 <u>Describe Routing Concepts</u>

Routers are primarily responsible for logical addressing and best path selection. They forward packets between different subnets, VLANs and across the WAN.

They build a routing table with routes comprised of network prefix, metric and next hop address. The router selects the route based on longest match rule and forwards packets to the next hop router (neighbor). There is support for load balancing, flow control and error recovery as well.

Each packet has a source and destination IP address. The router does a routing table lookup for a route to the destination subnet. The packet is then forwarded to the next hop address associated with the selected route.

Packet Handling Across the Network

ARP is a layer 3 network protocol that resolves a known IP address to an unknown MAC address. The local host must know the MAC address of the remote host before packets can be sent. That enables packet forwarding between local and remote host (server). The host checks the local ARP cache for an entry with the IP address and MAC address of a server. The host sends an ARP request to the default gateway if there is no local ARP entry. The default gateway (router) sends a proxy ARP broadcast and returns the MAC address for a server to the host In addition all routers between source and destination update their ARP table bindings (mappings). The switches note the server MAC address as well and update their MAC address table.

The output from **show arp** command lists the entries in the ARP cache table. The router adds the IP address and associated hardware (MAC) address for each ARP request to the cache.

The Aging field with (-) indicates the MAC address of the interface (Gi0/0) on Router-1. It does not age out from the table. The default ARP entry aging timer is 240 minutes. At that point the entry is flushed and new ARP request is required. The interface field signifies where the MAC address was learned. The serial interfaces do not have a MAC address.

router# **show arp**

Protocol	Address	Aging (min)	Hardware Address	Type	Interface
Internet	172.16.1.3	-	0000.000c.cccc	ARPA	GigabitEthernet0/0
Internet	172.16.1.2	12	0000.000b.bbbb	ARPA	GigabitEthernet0/0
Internet	172.16.1.1	12	0000.000a.aaaa	ARPA	GigabitEthernet0/0
Internet	172.16.2.2	12	0000.000d.dddd	ARPA	
Internet	172.16.3.1	12	0000.1234.5678	ARPA	

The source and destination MAC address are updated by routers as frames are forwarded between routers. The source MAC address is the router egress interface and destination MAC address is the neighbor ingress interface.

The forwarding decisions for routers are based on destination IP address and not destination MAC address. The source and destination IP address do not change between source and destination hosts.

Any layer 3 device such as a host or a router will write an IP header to create a packet with the source IP address and destination IP address.

The IP header has a field called Time-to-Live (TTL) that has a default value of 255. The purpose of TTL is to prevent packets from infinitely looping as a result of a routing loop. The TTL field is decremented by one with each router hop. That guarantees the packet will be discarded after 255 hops.

ARP for Default Gateway

Refer to the network drawing. Host-1 is establishing an initial connection to Server-1. The host sends an ARP broadcast for the MAC address of the default gateway if it isn't in the host ARP cache. It is the default gateway (router) that eventually does a proxy ARP request for the server MAC address.

Host-1 sends a layer 2 ARP broadcast frame on the local VLAN to request the MAC address of the default gateway. That is required before sending an ARP request to the default gateway router for the MAC address of Server-1.

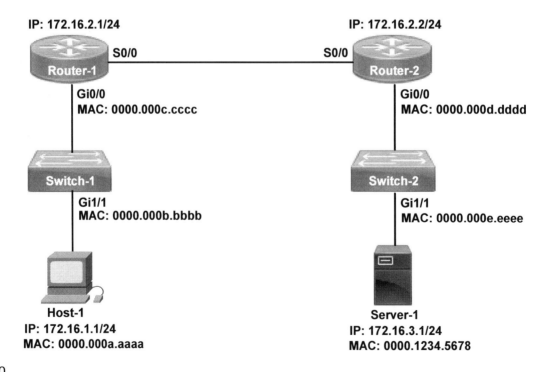

IP: 172.16.2.1/24
S0/0
Router-1
Gi0/0
MAC: 0000.000c.cccc
Switch-1
Gi1/1
MAC: 0000.000b.bbbb
Host-1
IP: 172.16.1.1/24
MAC: 0000.000a.aaaa

IP: 172.16.2.2/24
S0/0
Router-2
Gi0/0
MAC: 0000.000d.dddd
Switch-2
Gi1/1
MAC: 0000.000e.eeee
Server-1
IP: 172.16.3.1/24
MAC: 0000.1234.5678

The following describes the network addressing of the broadcast packet sent from Host-1 to start an initial session with Server-1.

- source MAC address = 0000.000a.aaaa
- destination MAC address = ffff.ffff.ffff
- source IP address = 172.16.1.1/24
- destination IP address = 172.16.3.1/24

Forwarding Decision Based on Route Lookup

The router builds a routing table with multiple routes (prefixes). The routes are assigned an administrative distance and metric cost.

Route Selection:

The administrative distance is a value assigned to a routing protocol. Metric is a path cost assigned to a specific route. The administrative distance and metric assigned to a route **will determine what route is installed in the routing table**.

The router installs the route with the lowest administrative distance including connected, static and default routes. In this example EIGRP has the lowest administrative distance and would be installed in the routing table.

- OSPF: 172.16.1.0/24
- RIPv2: 172.16.1.0/24
- **EIGRP (Internal): 172.16.1.0/24**

The route with the lowest metric is installed when there are multiple routes from the *same* routing protocol to the same destination. Equal cost load balancing is enabled when the route metrics to the same destination are equal. Administrative distance is configurable as well to influence route selection.

The following is an example of multiple routes from different routing protocols with different subnet mask (prefix) lengths. As a result they are all considered to be different destinations and all are installed in the routing table.

- OSPF: 172.16.1.0/21
- RIPv2: 172.16.1.0/23
- EIGRP: 172.16.1.0/27

Packet Forwarding:

The longest match rule is used to **select a route already installed in the routing table** as a forwarding decision. Each route has a specific prefix (subnet mask) length. The route with the longest prefix is selected from multiple routes within the same subnet range. For instance 172.16.0.0/22 has a longer prefix than 172.16.0.0/18 and used to forward packets to that destination.

Example 1:

The following is a list of routes and options for packet handling of an incoming packet. The router would select route **192.168.1.0/28** based on the longest match rule for packet forwarding to destination subnet 192.168.1.10/30

A. 192.168.1.0/24

B. 192.168.1.0/26

C. 192.168.1.0/28

D. gateway of last resort

E. packet discarded

Example 2:

Router-1 must select a route to forward packets to 172.16.4.0/28 network. Select the routing method, next hop address and router interface based on the routing table exhibit?

router-1# **show ip route**

Codes: C - connected, S - static, R - RIP, M - mobile, B - BGP
D - EIGRP, EX - EIGRP external, O - OSPF, IA - OSPF inter area
N1 - OSPF NSSA external type 1, N2 - OSPF NSSA external type 2
E1 - OSPF external type 1, E2 - OSPF external type 2
o - ODR, P - periodic downloaded static route

Gateway of last resort is not set

```
     172.16.0.0/24 is variably subnetted, 4 subnets, 2 masks
C      172.16.1.0/24 is directly connected, GigabitEthernet0/0
C      172.16.200.0/30 is directly connected, Serial0/0
C      172.16.200.16/30 is directly connected, Serial0/1
D      172.16.200.32/30 [90/1234567] via 172.16.200.2, Serial0/0
                        [90/1234567] via 172.16.200.18, Serial0/1
D      172.16.2.0/27 [90/1234567] via 172.16.200.18, Serial0/1
D      172.16.4.0/27 [90/1463212] via 172.16.200.2, Serial0/0
R      172.16.4.0/26 [120/3] via 172.16.200.17, Serial0/2
```

A. EIGRP, 172.16.200.32/30, Serial0/0

B. Connected, 172.16.200.16/30, Serial0/1

C. Connected, 172.16.1.0/24, GigabitEthernet0/0

D. EIGRP, 172.16.4.0/27, Serial0/0

E. RIPv2, 172.16.4.0/26, Serial0/2

The router selects the route with the longest prefix (subnet mask length) where there are multiple routes to the same destination. It is referred to as the longest match rule. The following EIGRP route has the longest prefix (/27) to the destination 172.16.4.0 subnet. The next hop address to forward packets destined for 172.16.4.0 is 172.16.200.2 via S0/0 local interface.

D **172.16.4.0/27** [90/1463212] via 172.16.200.2, Serial0/0

The routes 172.16.4.0/26 (RIPv2) and 172.16.4.0/27 (EIGRP) have different prefix lengths so they are considered different destinations by router. The router will install multiple routes from different routing protocols as a result. The administrative distance only applies to routes with the same subnet and prefix length (same destination).

EIGRP Metrics

The route with lowest metric is selected when multiple routes exist to the same destination (172.16.3.0) with same prefix length (/24) from the same routing protocol.

The bandwidth and delay are EIGRP defaults used to calculate metric value for a link. The delay is a fixed value based on interface speed. The link bandwidth is not cumulative with EIGRP.

Refer to the network topology drawing. There are multiple paths from 172.16.3.0 (source) to 172.16.2.0 (destination). Each path between source and destination is comprised of multiple individual links. EIGRP examines the links and determines the lowest bandwidth link for each path. The path with highest bandwidth (lowest metric) from among all lowest bandwidth links is selected (bolded path).

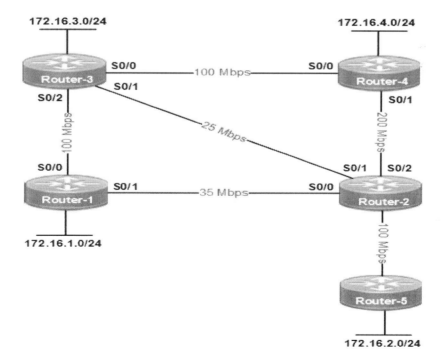

Router-3 -> Router-4 -> Router-2 -> Router-5 = 100 Mbps

Router-3 -> Router-1 -> Router-2 -> Router-5 = 35 Mbps

Router-3 -> Router-2 -> Router-5 = 25 Mbps

EIGRP Variance Command

EIGRP does support load balancing across unequal links to the same destination with the variance feature. The default for EIGRP is equal-cost (metric) load balancing.

The variance command allows for unequal cost load balancing between EIGRP enabled interfaces. The default is to forward traffic across the link with the lowest metric when there are multiple links to the same destination. The route has already been selected based on longest match rule.

EIGRP install all paths that have a metric less than the variance * the best metric in the routing table. The route must meet the feasibility condition to prevent routing loops. The feasibility condition states that, the Advertised Distance (AD) of a route must be lower than the feasible distance of the current successor route. Configuring variance by a factor of two instructs the router to include all routes less than 2 times the lowest metric. Note as well that the variance factor of two is the minimum.

RIPv2 Metrics

RIPv2 routes are selected based on the hop count only. The hop count is the number of routers between source and destination. The route with the lowest hop count to the destination is selected.

The maximum hop count (metric) for distance vector routing protocol RIPv2 is 15. That is the same maximum hop count as RIPv1. The packet is discarded at router hop 15.

RIPv2 does support load balancing across a maximum 4 paths between source and destination. The paths must have lowest and equal hop count to load balance packets.

OSPF Metrics

OSPF selects a path based on link cost (bandwidth) between source and destination. The cost of each link is calculated and added to arrive at a cumulative metric cost for the path. The minimum cost that can be assigned to any link is 1. The default OSPF reference bandwidth is 100 Mbps.

The following formula is used to calculate OSPF link cost.

cost = 100 Mbps / link bandwidth

Frame Rewrite

The source IP address and destination IP address does not change between network endpoints. The source MAC address and destination MAC address is rewritten at each layer 3 hop (router).

The local router updates (rewrite) source MAC address and destination MAC address in the frame header before forwarding the packet. The source MAC address is the local outbound router Ethernet interface. The destination MAC address is the MAC address of the next hop (neighbor) router Ethernet interface.

Serial interfaces do not have MAC addresses. As a result frame rewrite is assigned differently on serial point-to-point links. The router assigns the Ethernet interface where the frame was learned as source MAC address. In addition the router assigns the device MAC address assigned to the neighbor router as destination MAC address.

Frame Rewrite Examples

Example 1:

Refer to the network drawing. Host-1 has established a session with Server-1 and sending a new file. Host-1 sends all packets with the MAC address assigned to its network interface card as the source MAC address. The destination MAC address for the packet is the default gateway (router-1) Ethernet interface Gi0/0. That was obtained from the ARP request sent before the session started with Server-1. Switches forward frames and are never a destination.

- source MAC address as the packet leaves Host-1 = 0000.000a.aaaa
- destination MAC address as the packet leaves Host-1 = 0000.000c.cccc

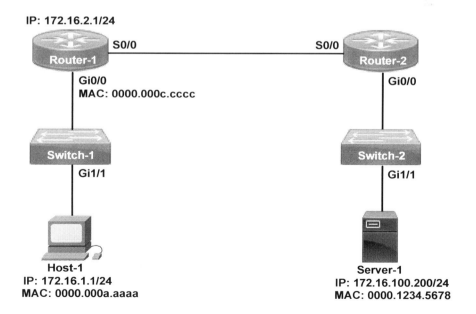

IP: 172.16.2.1/24

Router-1 S0/0 — S0/0 Router-2

Gi0/0
MAC: 0000.000c.cccc

Gi0/0

Switch-1

Gi1/1

Switch-2

Gi1/1

Host-1
IP: 172.16.1.1/24
MAC: 0000.000a.aaaa

Server-1
IP: 172.16.100.200/24
MAC: 0000.1234.5678

Example 2:

Refer to the network topology drawing. The router is the only network device that rewrites source and destination MAC address. The source MAC address is derived from the local router (Router-1) egress Ethernet interface.

The destination MAC address is derived from the next hop router (Router-2) ingress Ethernet interface. WAN serial interfaces do not have an assigned MAC address. As a result, Router-1 assigns the MAC address of the Ethernet interface (Gi0/0) where the packet was learned as source MAC address.

Router-1 assigns the MAC address of Router-2 Ethernet interface Gi0/0 as the destination MAC address. The MAC address of Router-2 is obtained from the router ARP table.

The source and destination MAC address of the packet at **P1** when it is forwarded to Router-2 is as follows:

- source MAC address = 0000.000c.cccc
- destination MAC address = 0000.000d.dddd

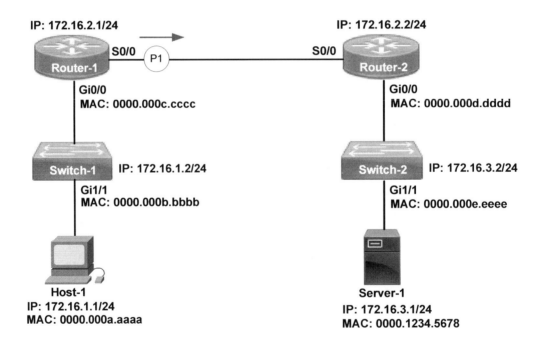

3.2 Interpret the Components of a Routing Table

Each routing table is comprised of multiple routes (entries). The router does a routing table lookup for the best route to the destination subnet. It is used for packet forwarding to the destination subnet.

1. Routing protocol code is the route source.
2. Destination subnet is the address of the remote network.
3. Administrative distance is the trustworthiness of the route source.
4. Metric is the path cost to the destination subnet.
5. Next hop is the interface of a neighbor router specified with a route.
6. Local interface is the exit interface used to forward packet to next hop address.

Example:

O   192.168.12.236 /30 [110/128] via 192.168.12.233, 00:35:36, Serial0/0

- Routing protocol code = O (OSPF)
- Destination subnet (prefix) = 192.168.12.236 /30
- Administrative distance = 110
- Metric = 128
- Next hop address = 192.168.12.233
- Local egress interface = Serial0/0

Routing Protocol Codes

The output of **show ip route** command lists the available routes. The protocol code assigned to the route signifies the source where the route was learned.

Table 3-1 Routing Protocol Codes

EGP	E
EIGRP	D
Host (/32)	L
OSPF	O
Default Route	S*
Static Route	S

3.3 Describe Routing Table Selection Based on Multiple Routing Sources

The route with the lowest administrative distance will be installed in the routing table. For instance EIGRP (90) has a lower administrative distance than OSPF (110) and RIPv2 (120). The result is the EIGRP route is installed in the routing table. The static route with administrative distance of 255 is not installed in the routing table.

Table 3-2 Administrative Distances for Routing Protocols

Directly Connected	0
Static Route	1
eBGP	20
EIGRP (Internal)	90
OSPF	110
RIPv2	120
External EIGRP	170

3.4 Configure, Verify and Troubleshoot InterVLAN Routing

Router-on-a-Stick

Refer to the network drawing. Host-1 and Server-1 are on different subnets. As a result routing is required to forward packets between the subnets. Layer 2 switches do not provide routing services or proxy ARP.

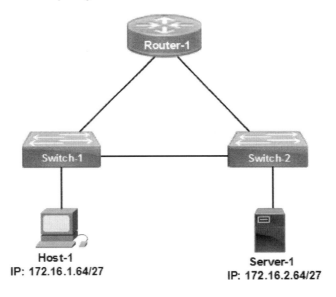

In addition Switch-1 has no default gateway configured and would discard all packets destined for a remote subnet. Assigning Host-1 and Server-1 to the same or different VLANs would not enable communication between them since they are not directly connected. The easiest solution to enable communication between different VLANs on each switch is router-on-a-stick. The alternative is a layer 3 switch configured with SVIs.

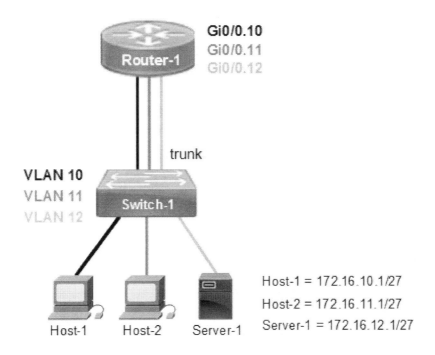

Host-1 = 172.16.10.1/27
Host-2 = 172.16.11.1/27
Server-1 = 172.16.12.1/27

Configuration

The following steps are required to configure router-on-a-stick

1. Configure trunk mode on switch uplink to router and allow VLANs.

2. Configure sub-interfaces on router with dot1q encapsulation for each VLAN

3. Configure each subinterface with an IP address in the same subnet as host VLAN.

Verify

The following show commands are all options to verify the subnet assigned to each VLAN on the router subinterface.

- show ip route
- show running-config
- show protocols

Troubleshooting InterVLAN Routing

The following are some common causes of InterVLAN errors.

- incorrect VLAN encapsulation on subinterface
- incorrect subnet mask assigned to subinterface
- trunk mode not enabled on switch uplink port

Switch Virtual Interface (SVI)

Switch-2 is a layer 2 device and has no routing (layer 3 forwarding) enabled. The switch makes forwarding decisions based on the destination MAC address.

Network management access (Telnet/SSH) to a switch requires a default gateway on the switch. The purpose of a default gateway is to forward packets destined for remote subnets to an upstream router. In addition the switch must be configured with an SVI for Layer 3 connectivity

- The switch is configured with **ip default-gateway** command
- The switch is configured with a Layer 3 VLAN interface called an SVI
- The VLAN interface is assigned an IP address for layer 3 connectivity
- The Telnet session from a host or router connects to the SVI address

The switch forwards any packets that are not on the local subnet to the default gateway (router). The host for instance is on a remote subnet from where Telnet is initiated. The SVI management VLAN must be assigned to the same subnet as the default gateway (router) interface.

> switch(config)# **ip default-gateway 192.168.1.254**
> switch(config)# **interface vlan 100**
> switch(config-if)# **ip address 192.168.1.2 255.255.255.0**
> switch(config-if)# **no shutdown**

3.5 <u>Compare and Contrast Static Routing and Dynamic Routing</u>

The static route is a manually configured route added to the routing table. It has an administrative distance of 1 making it a preferred route over all dynamically learned routes. The static route is configured from global configuration mode. The next hop to a destination subnet is configured as an IP address or local exit interface.

- The two advantages of static routes are security and minimal router CPU processing. The static routes are manually configured, enabled and managed by the network administrator. Route selection and forwarding packets to the destination subnet is deterministic.

70

- Dynamic routing protocols have security vulnerabilities that make them less desirable when connecting firewalls for instance. In addition dynamic routing protocols require more CPU utilization for hello packets, route calculation, convergence and routing updates.

3.6 <u>Compare Distance Vector and Link-State Routing Protocols</u>

- Routing protocols are either link-state or distance vector. The distance vector protocol assigns metric based on hop count. The best path selected has least number of hops.

- Link-state routing protocols discover the routing topology for enabled links and calculate the shortest (best) path. In addition they only send event-triggered routing updates. For instance a link failure on a router would trigger a routing reconvergence. They advertise classless routes as a default and automatic summarization is disabled. Classless routing protocols advertise the subnet in routing updates

- The router running a distance vector routing protocol will send routing table updates at regular intervals to neighbors. In addition the routing table is updated based on route advertisements from neighbors. The distance vector routing protocol is RIPv2.

- The purpose of split horizon is to prevent routing loops. It is enabled as a feature of distance vector routing protocols. It prevents routes from being advertised on the same interface where they were learned.

- The purpose of route poisoning is to prevent routing loops. It is a feature of distance vector routing protocols. The hop count for a route is increased so it is larger than the maximum supported. The router advertises the route to a neighbor as unreachable.

The following summarizes the differences between distance vector and link-state routing protocols.

Distance Vector Routing Protocols

- RIPv2, EIGRP
- Metric = distance based on hop count
- Regular routing table updates to neighbors
- Slower network convergence
- Small network
- Not scalable

Link-State Routing Protocols

- OSPF, IS-IS
- Metric = path cost
- Event-triggered routing updates
- Global topology database
- Scalable

3.7 Compare and Contrast Interior and Exterior Routing Protocols

Interior gateway routing protocols (IGP) advertise routes between routing domains that are privately managed. The IGP routing protocols include RIPv2, OSPF and EIGRP. BGP is an exterior routing protocol that enables routing across external routing domains managed by service providers (ISP).

3.8 Configure, Verify and Troubleshoot IPv4 and IPv6 Static Routing

Default Route

The default route is referred to as gateway of last resort packet forwarding. Any route, where no match exists, is forwarded to the default route next hop address. In the context of a router, the default route is often configured to forward packets to the internet. The administrative distance of a default route is 1 (the same as a static route).

The default route enables connectivity to the internet with a single route in the routing table. That minimizes the routing table size and router CPU utilization. Route processing and forwarding is offloaded to the internet service provider.

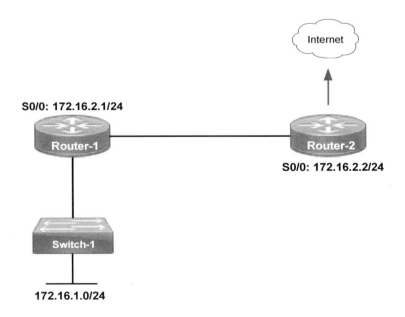

Packets arriving at Router-1 will use the default route when there is no route in the routing table. The default route will forward all packets with an unknown destination to the next hop address (172.16.2.2/24). It is referred to as *Gateway of Last Resort* on a router. The router will discard the packet when there is no destination route in the routing table and no default route is configured. In addition an ICMP **destination unreachable** error message is sent to the source.

> router-1(config)# **ip route 0.0.0.0 0.0.0.0 172.16.2.2**

Static Route

The static route is more specific than a default route.

- The static route says - *to reach this destination subnet forward packets to this next hop address or interface.*

- The default route says - *forward all traffic to this next hop when there is no route to the destination subnet in the routing table.*

- The specific subnet would use the next hop as neighbor network interface IP address or local router interface. Static routes are required at both routers as well to route (forward) in both directions.

  > static route on Router-1 with next hop 192.168.1.2/30 to Router-2
  > static route on Router-2 with next hop of 192.168.1.1/30 to Router-1

All packets to destination subnet 172.33.64.0 are forwarded to next hop 172.33.1.2

> router-1(config)# **ip route 172.33.64.1 255.255.255.224 172.33.1.2**

Static Route Advantages

- increased security with managed route updates and routing table changes
- bandwidth utilization is reduced with static routes
- deterministic routing

The disadvantages are less scalable and cause problems with network convergence that affect routing operations.

IPv6 Static Route

The following IOS commands configure an IPv6 static route with next hop as an interface. The router forwards all packets out the local egress interface (Gi0/0).

> router# **ipv6 route 2001:DB8:3C4D:1::/64 gigabitethernet 0/0**

The other option for configuring an IPv6 static route include the next hop IPv6 address fully specified to send across a broadcast network. The egress interface must be specified when the next hop is a link-local IPv6 address.

Table 3-3 IPv6 Route Types and Examples

network prefix	/64
default route	ipv6 route ::/0 2001:DB8:3C4D:1::1
WAN point-to-point serial link	/126
floating static route	ipv6 route ::/0 2001:DB8:3C4D:1::3/64 200
fully specified static route	ipv6 route 2001:DB8:3C4D:1::0/64 serial1/0 FE80::CA0A:01FF:33A9:1
host route	/128
directly connected static route	ipv6 route 2001:DB8::/32 serial 1/0

Floating Static Route

The purpose is to provide a redundant (backup) route when the static route is not available as a result of a failed link. The floating static route is assigned an administrative distance higher than one (static route default).

The following IOS command will configure a backup static route (floating) on router-1 to subnet 192.168.3.0/24 with an administrative distance of 200.

router-1(config)# **ip route 192.168.3.0 255.255.255.0 192.168.2.2 200**

- destination subnet = 192.168.3.0
- subnet mask = 255.255.255.0 (/24)
- next hop IP address = 192.168.2.2
- administrative distance = 200

Traffic destined for subnet 192.168.3.0 is forwarded to next hop 192.168.2.2. The administrative distance is a local value that affects what route is installed in the routing table. The default administrative distance for a static route is 1. Assigning a value of 200 to the static route makes it a floating static route.

3.9 Configure, Verify and Troubleshoot Single and Multi-Area OSPFv2

OSPF is a link-state routing protocol that builds and maintains a topology database. It is created with the exchange of hello packets and LSAs between routers. The link type along with path cost are used for selecting the shortest path to a destination subnet. They are the routes installed in the routing table and designated as best path routes. There is no exchange of routing tables at specific intervals as with distance vector protocols (RIPv2). OSPF sends event-triggered updates only such as when a link failure occurs to conserve bandwidth.

The OSPF design is characterized by well-defined hierarchical layers that enable route summarization and smaller routing tables per router. The routing updates are minimized when there are link failures enabling faster convergence. In addition routing issues such as flapping and routing loops are limited to an OSPF area.

OSPF is based on defining areas that create a hierarchical traffic flow for routing packets. There is a mandatory common backbone **area 0** that all other areas must connect to the backbone area. That is required to advertise LSAs between areas

The IOS command **show ip ospf database** provides a list of all known link states for an OSPF enabled network. It creates a network topology used to calculate best path (shortest) to a destination. The network topology and path cost for each link is considered as part of the calculation. The routing table is updated with the destination subnet and preferred next hop address.

OSPF Packet Types:

- Hello = neighbor discovery/adjacencies

- Database Descriptor = summarizes database topology

- Link-State Request = LSA request from neighbors

- Link-State Update = flooding LSAs to neighbors

- Link-State ACK = acknowledges LSA updates

Metric Calculation

Each routing protocol has a unique method for calculating route metric (cost). OSPF calculates cost based on link bandwidth. The default cost of an OSPF enabled Fast Ethernet link = 1 (100 Mbps/100 Mbps).

cost = 100 Mbps / link bandwidth

The lowest link cost assignable to a link is 1 even though the calculation could arrive at a lower number. The reference bandwidth is configurable for OSPF with the following IOS commands. This accounts for higher speed Ethernet interfaces that start at Gigabit (1000 Mbps) speed today. The reference bandwidth is a global configuration command that must match for all routers in the same OSPF routing domain.

```
router(config)# router ospf 1
router(config-router)# auto-cost reference-bandwidth 1000
```

The **ip ospf cost** command is an alternative to reference bandwidth method. It allows the network administrator to configure the cost directly on an interface. The third option is to manually change the interface speed with the interface **bandwidth** command.

Neighbor Adjacency

The purpose of hello packets are to discover neighbors and establish neighbor adjacencies. In addition hello packets are sent as keepalives to confirm the connected neighbor is still active.

OSPF enabled routers establish adjacencies with neighbors for communicating operational status and routing updates. The routing messages use timers that must match between directly connected neighbors. OSPF neighbor adjacencies are not formed when there is a mismatch of hello or dead timers. The following describe some additional reasons why neighbor adjacency would not occur between neighbors.

Adjacency States

The following is correct sequence of states for OSPF routers to establish adjacency. The command **show ip ospf neighbor** lists adjacency state with all neighbors.

1. **Down:** No hello packets received from neighbor

2. **Attempt:** Hello packet has not been received from NBMA neighbor where configured. The local router sends a hello packet to neighbor.

3. **Init:** Hello packet is received from neighbor. Local router verifies neighbor settings such as hello/dead timers and subnet mask are matching.

4. **Two-Way:** Hello packet received from neighbor with router ID of local router listed and DR/BDR election occurs for initial adjacency.

5. **Exstart:** DR starts exchanging link-state advertisements. The router with the higher router ID is assigned as master. The master router manages database synchronization to neighbor/s (slave).

6. **Exchange:** Routers exchange database descriptor packets (DBD).

7. **Loading:** Routers exchange all link-state information (LSA).

8. **Full:** Normal state where adjacency is established between neighbors.

OSPF Hello Packets

The hello packet advertises various OSPF configuration settings between adjacent neighbors. In addition it detects the operational status of a neighbor. Any routes advertised from a neighbor with the interface down are deleted from the routing table. Neighbor adjacency is not permitted between settings that must match such as timers and common interface subnet. The following setting are advertised in hello packets.

- hello timer and dead timer (sec)
- router priority
- DR/BDR assigned to local segment
- area assigned to neighbor interface
- subnet mask of neighbor interface
- authentication method

OSPF Designated Router

OSPF designated routers (DR) advertise routing updates to connected spokes on a shared network segment (Ethernet). The purpose is to minimize route updates.

The DR is a hub and advertises route updates to 224.0.0.6 multicast address. Any connected spoke routers on the local segment will receive multicasts of the route updates. The OSPF router with the highest priority is elected as DR for the network segment (subnet). The router priority is configurable as well to influence the DR election. Where equal priorities exist, the OSPF router with higher router ID is elected, then higher loopback address, then higher physical interface number.

router-1# **show ip ospf neighbor**

Neighbor_ID	Pri	State	Dead Time	Address	Interface
172.16.254.1	1	Full/DR	00:00:12	172.16.1.2	GigabitEthernet0/0
172.16.254.2	1	Full/DR	00:00:13	172.16.1.1	GigabitEthernet0/1
172.16.1.1	1	Full/BDR	00:00:12	172.16.1.25	GigabitEthernet0/1

Router-1 is a spoke connected to two different designated routers (DR) shown with 2 x FULL/DR states. Router-1 has two Ethernet interfaces with a unique DR router connected to each segment (switch). The DR election is per network segment. The elected DR router would have FULL/DROTHER state for each connected spoke. The results of **show ip ospf neighbor** command lists the following OSPF neighbor status:

- Neighbor_ID = neighbor router ID
- Pri = neighbor priority
- State = neighbor DR/BDR/DROTHER status
- Dead Time = dead timer age
- Address = neighbor connected router interface IP address
- Interface = neighbor connected router interface

Example:

Refer to the network drawing. All routers are configured with the default OSPF priority. What router will be elected designated router (DR) for Router-1?

The default OSPF configuration has no router ID assigned. In addition the OSPF priority has a default value of 1. OSPF assigns the highest IP address of any existing Loopback address for the router ID for that segment. That occurs only when there isn't any manual configuration of router ID. The highest IP address of any active physical interface is assigned if no Loopback interface exists. The router ID is advertised with Type 1 (Router) LSAs.

The switches create two separate network segments for OSPF multicasting. As a result the designated Router (DR) for Router-1 is Router-4 with router ID (RID) of **172.16.4.1**. Router-5 is on a separate network segment connected to Switch-2 and not assignable to routers on Switch-1.

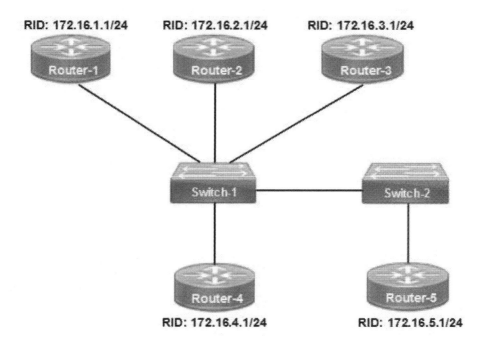

The highest IP address is calculated from left to right and based on IP address numbering. The numbers for each IP address match until octet 3 where subnet 4 is higher. That is the IP address assigned to Router-4.

- 172.16.1.1
- 172.16.2.1
- 172.16.3.1
- 172.16.**4**.1

Correct Answer: **Router-4**

Any OSPF enabled router with a priority of zero (0) cannot be elected as the designated router (DR) or BDR. The following command assigns a priority of zero (0) to a router.

    router(config-if)# **ip ospf priority 0**

OSPF Operation

- The OSPF process ID is a unique number assigned to an OSPF routing instance. It is only locally significant to the router. The valid range for a process ID is 1 - 65,535. The routing instance includes a separate OSPF topology database for each process ID.

- Cisco supports multiple OSPF instances per router defined with a process identifier. It is similar to a VRF where a routing instance is created for a specific purpose such as partner connectivity. There is a maximum of 32 processes permitted per router. Any OSPF interface can only be assigned to a single process identifier.

- All OSPF routers send hello packets to neighbors on the same segment (subnet) using multicast 224.0.0.5 as the destination IP address.

- All areas must be connected directly to the backbone (area 0). The virtual link is not required where there is only a single area. It connects an area to the backbone area through an already connected area.

- The default hello timer interval for a multi-access (broadcast) network is 10 seconds. The dead timer is a default of 4 times the hello interval. Ethernet is an example of a multi-access network type.

- There is no maximum hop count for OSPF so it is unlimited.

- Passive interfaces prevent local router from sending hello message routing update on an interface to a non-OSPF neighbor. That provides security and minimize bandwidth utilization on links to non-OSPF neighbors.

Global Configuration

    router(config)# **router ospf** [process id]
    router(config-router)# **network** [ip address] [wildcard mask] **area** [number]

Verify OSPF

The following show commands verify OSPF operational status and layer 3 connectivity.

    router# **show ip ospf interfaces**

    router# **show ip ospf neighbor**

Troubleshooting OSPFv2

The following is a list of the most common causes of OSPF network errors. The result is no neighbor adjacency and as a result routes are not advertised.

- interfaces are shutdown
- area ID mismatch between neighbors
- hello and/or dead timer mismatch between neighbors
- OSPF network type mismatch between neighbors
- neighbor interfaces not assigned to the same subnet
- **network** command wildcard mask incorrect
- passive interface enabled on an interface

3.10 Configure, Verify and Troubleshoot Single and Multi-Area OSPFv3

There is no requirement for OSPFv3 neighbors to share the same subnet to form an adjacency. OSPFv3 neighbor adjacency is established with link-local address. OSPFv3 routing is per link instead of per subnet with multiple instances per link support.

OSPFv2

- Assigned to a subnet
- Single IP address per interface
- IPv4 addressing only
- Multicast 224.0.0.5 (all OSPF SPF routers) / 224.0.0.6 (DR/BDR)

OSPFv3

- Multiple IPv6 addresses per interface
- Adjacencies over link-local IP address
- IPv4 and IPv6 addressing
- FF02::5 (all OSPF SPF routers) / FF02::6 (all DR/BDR routers)

OSPFv3 Configuration

The following assigns a global routable ipv6 address to an interface. The *eui-64* keyword converts the address to modified format where the MAC address is used to create a unique interface id. The interface is assigned process ID 1 and area 0.

```
router(config)# interface gigabitethernet0/0
router(config-if)# no ip address
router(config-if)# ipv6 enable
router(config-if)# ipv6 address 2001:AB3E::/64 eui-64
router(config-if)# ospfv3 1 ipv6 area 0
```

3.11 Configure, Verify and Troubleshoot EIGRP for IPv4

Autonomous System (AS)

The single EIGRP autonomous system (AS) design simplifies routing significantly. The result is less router processing for a single EIGRP instance. The configuration is less complex and route propagation is automatic within a single AS. Route redistribution is required between multiple AS when deployed. EIGRP enabled routers can only advertises routes within the same autonomous system (AS). As a result the AS number assigned to each router must match.

Convergence

EIGRP is similar to OSPF where there is a routing table, neighbor table and topology table. Feasible successors are backup routes stored in the topology table.

Neighbor Table = directly connected EIGRP neighbors

Topology Table = routes learned from EIGRP neighbors including feasible successors.

Routing Table = best (successor) routes selected from the EIGRP topology table.

The following table correctly describe the EIGRP route types available.

Table 3-4 EIGRP Route Types

EIGRP Successor	best advertised route to a destination subnet. It is the route in the routing table
EIGRP AD	advertised cost from an EIGRP neighbor to the destination subnet
EIGRP Feasible Successor	backup route with advertised distance less than the feasible distance of the current successor route
EIGRP FD	advertised distance (cost) + cost between the local router and the next-hop router

The following correctly describes EIGRP operation with default settings.

- EIGRP only uses a backup route if the advertised distance (AD) is less than the feasible distance (FD).

- The backup route selection rule prevents routing loops.

- Turn off auto summarization when classless subnet masks are configured.

Holddown Timer

EIGRP holddown timer affects how fast the network converges when there is a link failure. Each router interface enabled with EIGRP sends hello packets to its EIGRP neighbors. The default holddown timer value expires after three hello packets are not received from a neighbor. That is the time interval that EIGRP waits before declaring the neighbor unreachable. The local router notifies the neighbor that it is dropping the neighbor adjacency with a goodbye message.

Verify EIGRP Adjacency

The following command is used to confirm all established EIGRP adjacencies and IP addressing for the local router. It lists the active EIGRP neighbor adjacencies along with IP address and operational status. The smooth round trip time (SRTT), retransmit timeout setting (RTO) and queue count are included.

> router# **show ip eigrp neighbor**

Troubleshooting EIGRP

The following is a list of the most common causes of EIGRP network errors. The result is EIGRP neighbor adjacencies are not formed and routes are not advertised.

- network interface is shutdown
- autonomous system mismatch between neighbors
- K values mismatch between neighbor interfaces
- neighbor interfaces are not assigned to the same subnet
- **network** command is missing subnet address or advertising incorrect subnet
- **network** command is configured with incorrect subnet mask
- passive interface enabled

The network interfaces on point-to-point link are not in the same subnet as required by EIGRP. As a result the routers won't establish EIGRP neighbor adjacency.

3.12 Configure, Verify and Troubleshoot EIGRP for IPv6

EIGRP for IPv6 requires a router ID to be configured under the routing process. The EIGRP **router-id** command is used when no IPv4 address is enabled.

The support for IPv6 addressing with EIGRP includes the following new features:

- EIGRP is configured per interface
- no support for network statements
- protocol instance is not enabled until the router ID is configured

3.13 Configure, Verify and Troubleshoot RIPv2 for IPv4

- The primary enhancement to RIPv2 is support for classless subnets (CIDR). That enables advertisement of subnet mask length with routing advertisements.

- RIPv2 routes use MD5 authentication between routers for optimized security.

- RIPv2 sends routing table updates as a multicast to 224.0.0.9 instead of a broadcast used with RIPv1.

RIPv2 Configuration

The following commands will enable RIPv2 with classless routing

router(config)# **router rip**
router(config-router)# **version 2**
router(config-router)# **network 172.16.0.0**
router(config-router)# **no auto-summary**

Troubleshooting RIPv2

- interface is shutdown
- directly connected interfaces are not in same subnet
- **network** command has an incorrect subnet address or missing subnet
- **no auto-summary** command is not configured for classless routing

3.14 Troubleshoot Basic Layer 3 End-to-End Connectivity Issues

Standard OSI model troubleshooting methodology:

1. Ethernet Cabling
2. Network Interface Card
3. IP Addressing
4. DNS Server
5. Application

The operational status of router interfaces can be verified with the following commands:

router# **show interfaces**
router# **show ip interface brief**
router# **show protocols**

Show IP Interface Brief

The IOS command **show ip interface** brief provides interface and line protocol status. That include all network interfaces with an assigned IP address. The Status column is layer 1 Ethernet signaling while the Protocol column is layer 2 data link connectivity.

The network interface status becomes "administratively down" when the network administrator configures the **shutdown** command. It is an interface level IOS command that manually changes the interface to down.

The **show ip interface brief** command displays any unconfigured interfaces as an unassigned IP address with status of *down/down*. The normal status is an assigned IP address with status of *up/up*.

router-1# **show ip interface brief**

Interface	IP address	OK	Method	Status	Protocol
GigabitEthernet0/0	172.16.1.1	YES	NVRAM	up	down
GigabitEthernet0/1	172.16.2.1	YES	Manual	up	up
Serial0/0	172.16.3.1	YES	Manual	up	up
Serial0/1	Unassigned	YES	Unset	admin down	down
Loopback0	172.16.1.254	YES	NVRAM	up	up

The **NVRAM** status for GigabitEthernet0/0 indicates an interface change was made to the startup configuration file. For instance the IP address and subnet mask was assigned to the interface.

In addition the router was reloaded at some point after the configuration. The *Manual* status indicates some configuration change occurred and currently active however the router was not reloaded yet.

The following summarizes standard troubleshooting commands for verifying and troubleshooting layer 3 connectivity:

Table 3-5 Standard Layer 3 Troubleshooting Commands

show interfaces	interface operational status, IP address, MAC address, MTU, bandwidth and interface errors
show ip interface brief	layer 1 and layer 2 interface status, all enabled interfaces
Ping	verify layer 3 reachability to a remote peer interface
show protocols	interface status, IP address and subnet mask
show running-config	verify the device configuration is correct

ICMP *destination host unreachable* message is returned by a router to host. The message indicates that router cannot forward packets from that point. The cause could include physical (layer 1), encapsulation (layer 2), routing (layer 3) or ACL filtering.

Host Addressing

The Windows command **ipconfig /all** is used for troubleshooting desktop connectivity issues. The output displays host IPv4/IPv6 addressing and that DHCP has assigned the default gateway. In addition the network administrator can verify the MAC address and operational status of all network adapters. Any issues with network connectivity from the client side can be confirmed.

Troubleshooting Host Connectivity

- incorrect default gateway
- incorrect subnet
- DHCP not enabled
- incorrect DNS server

Subnet Mismatch

Refer to the network topology drawing. What is the best explanation for why Host-1 cannot ping Server-1?

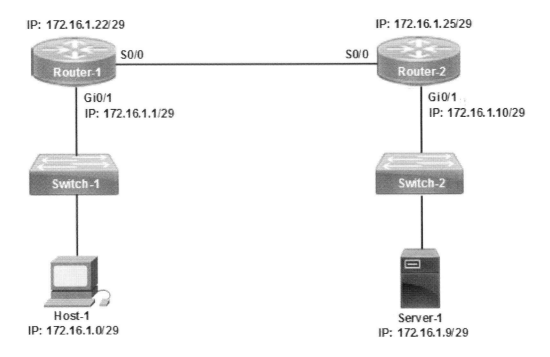

A. Host-1 and Server-1 are not on the same subnet

B. routing is not enabled on any switch

C. serial interfaces are assigned to different subnets

D. IP address of Server-1 is incorrect

Correct Answer (C)

The physical network interfaces for directly connected links must be assigned to the same subnet. That applies to LAN or WAN interfaces. The subnet mask and subnet within that range determines the subnet assigned to the network interface. The number of subnets available is based on the subnet mask length.

> Router-1 = 172.16.1.22/29
> Router-2 = 172.16.1.25/29

The /29 subnet mask assigns 29 bits to the network portion and 3 bits ($2^3 = 8$) to the host portion. The number of host addresses assignable = 6 (8 - 2). The network address (zero) and broadcast address (all ones) cannot be assigned.

> network portion (/29) | hosts (1-6)
> **11111111.11111111.11111111.11111** 000

- Router-1 = 172.16.1.22/29
- Network address = 172.16.1.16/29
- Broadcast address = 172.16.1.23/29

- Router-2 = 172.16.1.25/29
- Network address = 172.16.1.24/29
- Broadcast address = 172.16.1.31/29

- IP subnet range 1 = 172.16.1.16 - 172.16.1.23
- IP subnet range 2 = 172.16.1.24 - 172.16.1.31

The result is that Router-1 is within IP subnet range 1 while Router-2 is within IP subnet range 2. The serial interfaces are assigned to different subnets and can't communicate. The ping is discarded and *destination host unreachable* is returned by Router-1.

4.0 WAN Technologies

4.1 Configure and Verify PPP and MLPPP WAN Connectivity

The following describe the standard reasons for deploying WAN connectivity:

- enable connectivity between branch offices, data center and cloud
- information sharing among internal and external organizations

Serial Interfaces

Serial interfaces connect devices that are assigned as a DCE or DTE. The DCE provides clocking for the serial interface. The DTE is the device receiving the clock signal. The router is a DTE that connects to a DCE such as CSU/DSU or DSL modem.

DTE - DCE - **[DCE ISP DCE]** - DCE - DTE

The CSU/DSU terminates the digital local loop from the service provider network (ISP). Analog interfaces terminate an analog local loop and converts between digital and analog signaling. The Cisco default synchronous serial interface encapsulation type is HDLC. Verify WAN encapsulation with **show interfaces** command.

TCP-based applications require a three-way handshake for host-to-host connectivity.

1. host sends TCP SYN message to server with bit set
2. server sends TCP SYN/ACK message to host with bit set for both
3. host sends message to server with TCP ACK bit set

Point-to-Point Protocol (PPP)

The maximum speed supported on a single PPP link is T1/E1 however MLPPP enables bundling for increased bandwidth. Encapsulation must match between peering routers configured with PPP.

- LCP is a Layer 2 protocol that establishes, manage and terminates the WAN connection.

- LCP negotiates PAP/CHAP authentication with the remote peer router.

- NCP provides protocol encapsulation for multiple layer 3 network protocols that are configured.

The normal operational status for LCP (layer 2) is *Open* when the PPP link is working correctly. In addition NCP, IPCP and Multilink interface also show as *Open*.

IPCP is the Network Control Protocol (NCP) for IPv4 traffic across a PPP link. The client IP address request is processed through IPCP for a PPP link. In addition IPCP allows for requesting the IP address from a DHCP server.

PPP Configuration

The following IOS commands will enable PPP on serial interface 1/0/0 with CHAP authentication and password *cisco*.

router(config)# **interface serial1/0/0**
router(config-if)# **encapsulation ppp** *(enables PPP)*
router(config-if)# **ppp authentication chap** *(enables CHAP)*
router(config-if)# **ppp chap password cisco** *(password = cisco)*
router(config-if)# **ppp chap hostname WAN-Router** *(hostname* = WAN-Router*)*

CHAP/PAP Authentication

CHAP/PAP are authentication protocols that provides secure authentication across PPP/MLPPP serial interfaces. The authentication requires passwords and hostnames to match between local and remote peering routers.

- The number of retry attempts is controlled by the peer router. Messages are sent periodically to verify the peering device is authentic.

- There is no hashing available with PAP authentication. The username and password is sent as clear text only.

The following configures CHAP authentication with PAP as the fallback protocol:

router(config-if)# **ppp authentication chap pap**

Local Authentication

The first command **aaa authentication ppp default local** enables use of the local username database for authenticating the peer router.

The second command **ppp authentication pap chap** enables PAP and CHAP authentication. The router will attempt PAP authentication first and then fallback to CHAP based on the configuration order.

router(config)# **aaa authentication ppp default local**
router(config-if)# **ppp authentication pap chap**

Multilink PPP (MLPPP)

Multilink PPP (MLPPP) enables bundling of multiple links into a single logical link. That includes encapsulation of serial or broadband (Ethernet/DSL) WAN services. There is a limit of 10 links per serial bundle and 8 link per Ethernet/DSL bundle.

- interface multilink 10 *(assigns bundle number)*
- ip address 172.16.1.1 255.255.0.0
- no keepalive
- ppp multilink *(enables multilink)*
- ppp multilink group 10 *(allow only physical link assigned to bundle 10)*

Verify MLPPP

The following command will verify the interface status and encapsulation type for Multilink bundle 1.

router# **show interfaces multilink 1**

The following command displays the status of all bundle member (physical) interfaces. In addition any interface errors are listed as well.

router# **show ppp multilink**

Link Quality Monitoring

The purpose of Link Quality Monitoring (LQM) is to detect packet drop errors on a PPP WAN link. It provides error detection and correction across the PPP link. The link quality report packet (LQR) is sent across the WAN at regular intervals. The LQR calculates the percentage of packets transmitted from packets that were received. It is disabled by default however is configurable with the **ppp quality [percent]** command.

Troubleshooting PPP/MLPPP

- IP address and/or subnet mask is misconfigured on an interface
- static route *next hop address* does not point to the remote tunnel interface
- CHAP password and hostname mismatch with peering neighbor
- encapsulation type mismatch

The command **show ppp multilink** is used to verify all active member links of a multilink bundle. It confirms the multilink interface is up and forwarding packets. In addition the bundle name is listed and number of packet drops.

The command **debug ppp negotiation** is used to troubleshoot PPP link errors. The output lists LCP link establishment and PAP/CHAP negotiation with the remote router. IPCP packets such as IP address requests are displayed as well.

Refer to the network topology drawing. Host-1 cannot send packets to Server-1. Select two possible causes based on the results of **show ip interface brief** command?

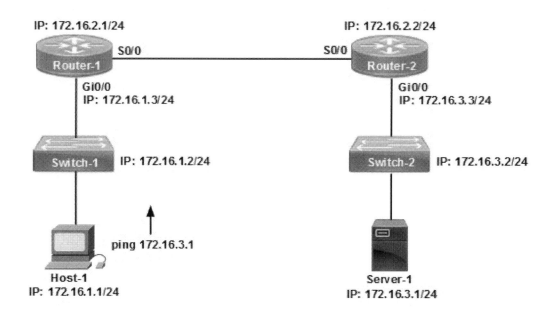

router-1# **show ip interface brief**

Interface	IP address	OK	Method	Status	Protocol
GigabitEthernet0/0	172.16.1.3	YES	NVRAM	up	up
GigabitEthernet0/1	Unassigned	YES	Manual	administratively down	down
Serial0/0	172.16.2.1	YES	Unset	up	down
Serial0/1	Unassigned	YES	Manual	administratively down	down

A. clocking error between routers
B. cabling issue
C. serial line encapsulation mismatch between routers
D. Router-2 interface Serial0/0 (S0/0) is administratively down
E. Router-1 is configured with the wrong subnet mask
F. Router-2 loopback is assigned the wrong subnet mask

Correct Answers (A,C)

The IOS command **show ip interface brief** displays the operational status for all network interfaces with an assigned IP address. The Status column is layer 1 Ethernet signaling while the Protocol column is layer 2 data link connectivity. Router-1 interface S0/0 (172.16.2.1) is **up/down** confirming the problem is line protocol (layer 2). Typical Layer 2 causes include clocking errors and encapsulation mismatch between routers.

4.2 Configure, Verify and Troubleshoot PPPoE Client-Side Interfaces

PPPoE was designed to encapsulate PPP frames inside Ethernet frames. PPP enables authentication, encryption and compression for PPPoE sessions across the internet. PPPoE over Ethernet client feature for Cisco routers has a client/server peering model.

The client router is at the customer premises and the server device is at the ISP. It is typically deployed for DSL connectivity from a Cisco router with Ethernet only interfaces. The DSL modem is connected to the Cisco router Ethernet interface.

The client mode router requests an IP address from the ISP with IPCP negotiation. In addition the client mode router negotiates authentication with the ISP server. PPPoE client mode enables multiple hosts on an Ethernet segment to access DSL services.

The following table compares PPP and PPPoE characteristics and usage.

Table 4-1 Comparing PPP and PPPoE feature characteristics

peer to peer	PPP
security features	PPP
serial lines	PPP
router	PPP
multipoint broadcast	PPPoE
easy to deploy	PPPoE
layer 2 transport independent	PPPoE
Ethernet only router	PPPoE
bridge	PPPoE

The PPPoE client is uniquely identified with a MAC address and session ID. There is a MAC address exchange between peers before NCP (layer 3) starts. That is required to identify the MAC address of the remote peer router.

The session ID is assigned to the PPPoE session after MAC address discovery. Peer authentication is negotiated during the PPPoE session phase.

The **interface dialer 1** command negotiates an IP address from the PPPoE server with IPCP. The virtual-template is configured on the PPPoE server to allocate IP addresses to clients. The command **pppoe-client dial-pool-number 1** binds the physical interface to the dialer interface on the PPPoE client.

Enable PPPoE

The following commands enable PPPoE on a client interface:

router (config-if)# **pppoe enable**
router (config-if)# **pppoe-client dial-pool-number 1**

4.3 Configure, Verify and Troubleshoot GRE Tunnel Connectivity

The purpose of GRE is to enable routing protocols across the WAN. It is typically deployed to support routing protocol advertisements across a VPN. That is accomplished by tunneling (encapsulating) the routing protocol.

The two primary advantages of GRE tunneling include the following:

- routing protocol support across the internet
- increase hop count for layer 3 protocols

Some advantages of GRE/DMVPN connectivity include the following:

- lower support costs and scalability
- tunnel multiple protocols across the internet
- increase the hop count where required
- dynamic VPN tunnel setup and configuration
- enable increased security with VPN encryption
- redundant (backup) tunnels across the internet

GRE assigns a tunnel source and tunnel destination IP address. They are public (NBMA) routable IP addresses. In addition the tunnel source address refers to a local interface. The tunnel destination address is the remote router interface.

- public routable IP address
- local router interface

Next Hop Resolution Protocol (NHRP) enables the dynamic tunnel setup between hub and spokes. There is an automatic detection of all spoke public IP addresses (NBMA). The public routable (tunnel source) IP address is dynamically assigned to the spoke (branch) by the ISP. The spoke registers the NBMA IP address with the hub router.

NHRP at the hub router maps the spoke tunnel source address to spoke tunnel interface. The tunnel interface (logical) is the private IP address. The hub router at the data center builds a table with mappings for all connected spoke routers. The tunnel interface is often a loopback address. Packet forwarding is enabled with next hop addressing (routes) between hub router and all connected spokes.

GRE is a stateless protocol with no flow control and assigned IP protocol 47. GRE tunneling provides no security at all for packets traversing the internet. IPsec provides encryption and authentication for GRE tunnels.

Refer to the network drawing. The GRE tunnel is configured with a Tunnel (virtual) interface and a public routable Tunnel source IP address is shown for each peering router.

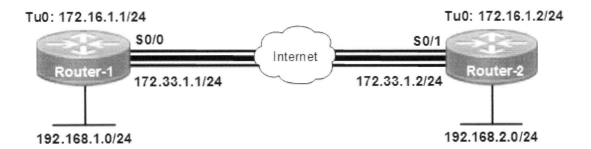

GRE Tunnel interface IP addresses are from the private network and not routable. They are assigned to the Tunnel interface on each router with a number. The network topology drawing assigned the following IP addresses to Tunnel0 (Tu0) interface.

     172.16.1.1/24 = Tunnel0 interface IP address (Router-1)
     172.16.1.2/24 = Tunnel0 interface IP address (Router-2)

GRE Tunnel source IP addresses are public routable and assigned by the ISP. They are assigned to the public facing physical interface on each router. The Tunnel source IP address assigned to the remote router is referred to as the Tunnel destination IP address. The network topology drawing assigned the following IP addresses.

     172.33.1.1/24 = GRE tunnel source IP address (Router-1)
     172.33.1.2/24 = GRE tunnel source IP address (Router-2)

The following command will enable GRE tunnel support across the DMVPN.

     router(config-if)# **tunnel mode gre multipoint**

The IOS command **show interface tunnel 1** is used to verify tunnel interface status (up/up), configured settings and performance. The **running-config** command is used to verify all GRE configuration and static routes. The next hop address of each local static route must point to the remote tunnel interface.

     router# **show interface tunnel 1**
     router# **show running-config**

4.4 Describe WAN Topology Options

1. *Point-to-Point* topology is used for direct connectivity of network devices.

2. *Hub and Spoke* is a star topology that provides connectivity to the hub and between endpoints (branch offices). The hub and spoke topology is deployed with DMPVN connectivity.

3. *Full Mesh* topology provides a link to and between all endpoints for any-to-any connectivity.

WAN homing describes the network topology between customer and ISP for internet access. In addition along with topology there are levels of redundancy. The following are correct statements concerning WAN homing topologies.

- dual homed provides link redundancy
- single homed provides no link redundancy
- dual homed provides two connections to same ISP

4.5 Describe WAN Access Connectivity Options

Multiprotocol Label Switching (MPLS)

MPLS is a layer 2.5 WAN transport solution that encapsulates layer 2 transport protocols. Internet routing is provided to customers across the MPLS network. MPLS segments customer traffic streams with a label and tag. The following are four standard advantages available with MPLS:

- multiprotocol transport
- IPv4 and IPv6 support
- any-to-any connectivity
- QoS support

Three advantages of DMVPN connectivity over traditional services:

- scalability
- increased security
- cost effective

Standard VPN services are characterized by the following attributes:

- privacy (data encryption)
- data integrity (hashing)
- authentication (RSA)

The following table summarizes characteristics of WAN access protocols:

Table 4-2 Characteristics of WAN Access Connectivity Protocols

SSL VPN	web-based encryption, dynamic, easy to deploy, granular application security
MPLS	branch office, multiprotocol support, WAN access solution, layer 2.5, layer 3 VPN
IPsec VPN	static VPN, private, point-to-point topology, difficult to deploy, router peering
DMVPN	internet-based VPN, layer 3, cloud connectivity, IWAN, dynamic
Metro Ethernet	easy to deploy, layer 2, bandwidth on demand, distance limits
PPPoE	internet-based, layer 2, DSL, cable, static configuration

4.6 Configure and Verify Single-Homed Branch Connectivity with eBGP

BGP is a routing protocol with connectivity based on TCP transport. The BGP router ID provides recovery from TCP session collisions. The highest loopback IP address is assigned as router ID by default.

The local router identify a BGP neighbor based on IP address and autonomous system number for peering purposes. BGP advertises routes based on the configured static routes (**ip route**) and the **network** command.

eBGP Configuration

The following commands will configure a BGP routing instance and assign it to AS 10. The **neighbor** command creates an eBGP session with the remote router based on the neighbor IP address 172.16.1.2 and AS 40. The **network** command advertises the specific subnet 10.10.34.1/24 to the BGP neighbor.

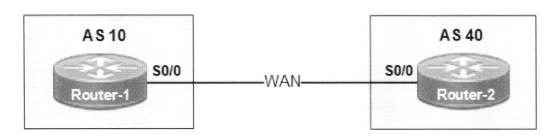

- enable BGP with local AS 10
- add eBGP peering neighbor from AS 40
- assign IP address 172.16.1.2 to remote peer
- advertise network 10.10.34.1/24 to remote peer

```
router(config)# router bgp 10
router(config-router)# neighbor 172.16.1.2 remote-as 40
router(config-router)# network 10.10.34.1 mask 255.255.255.0
```

The eBGP session is created when BGP routers assigned to different BGP autonomous systems (AS) are peering.

The **network** command advertises the network prefixes assigned. In addition the **network 0.0.0.0** command advertises the default route in the routing table. The BGP **network** command must match the route installed in the local routing table.

Verify eBGP Connectivity

The following command lists all BGP peers for the local router and neighbor adjacency state. The normal adjacency state is *Established* for a BGP session when routing updates are exchanged.

```
router# show ip bgp neighbors
```

The IOS command **show ip bgp summary** provides a quick summarized lists of all BGP neighbor connections. That includes BGP AS number and up/down connection status. In addition there is detailed memory usage and session activity listed.

```
router# show ip bgp summary
```

4.7 Describe Basic QoS Concepts

The following are primary reasons for deploying QoS on a network:

- guarantee SLAs for defined traffic classes
- avoid and manage network congestion
- prioritize traffic classes and assign bandwidth
- minimize packet loss and network latency

QoS is only applied when network congestion is detected. The purpose is to manage the available network bandwidth for optimizing network performance.

QoS techniques are enabled to decrease latency, packet loss and jitter. It is particularly significant to delay sensitive voice and video traffic.

Table 4-3 Characteristics of Standard QoS Techniques

class map	access groups, traffic matching
classification	class of service, DSCP, NBAR, access list
congestion avoidance	WRED, tail drop, thresholds
service-policy	attach policy to interface
bandwidth management	shaping, policing
policy map	traffic marking, point to class map
congestion management	FIFO, WFQ, PQ, CBWFQ (queuing)

Packet Marking

The only network interface that supports Class of Service (CoS) marking is an Ethernet switch trunk. The 802.1q tag is added to an Ethernet frame when trunking is enabled. The 802.1q field is used for VLAN membership tagging. That allows forwarding of multiple VLANs between switches. There is a 3 bit field used for CoS marking and prioritization (queuing) of traffic. Type of Service (ToS) is an 8-bit field in IP packet for DSCP packet marking

Class of Service (CoS)

Routers can only examine the CoS marking of a frame and trust or remark the layer 3 packet. The router would specifically strip off the original frame and rewrite MAC addressing. In addition the router would either trust the CoS value or rewrite a DSCP value equal to the CoS marking. Layer 2 switches are configured with a trust state that determines frame handling.

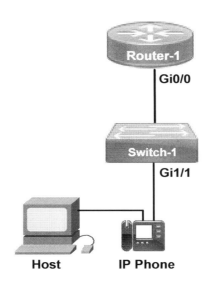

97

Cisco IP phones mark all voice traffic to the switch with default CoS 5. In addition a trunk is created from the IP phone to the switch when the voice VLAN feature is enabled. The trunk tags voice packets from the phone and data from the host to an access port on the switch.

Trust State

The trust state of a switch determines how the packet marking is interpreted for ingress traffic. The default trust setting for a Cisco switch is *untrusted*. The switch will remark the CoS or DSCP value to zero (0) for all ingress packets on an untrusted interface.

The switch will examine an ingress packet and forward it unaltered when trust state is enabled. For instance voice packets marked as Cos 5 from an IP phone are forwarded with that value. Packets from a host are remarked from a default zero (0) to a configured value on a trusted interface.

Defining trust boundaries across the network topology affects how packets markings are processed. All network devices within a trust boundary won't remark packets as they traverse. The following are key points for QoS trust boundary configuration.

- packets from a trusted device are not remarked on upstream device
- trust boundary defines the point where trusted packets start
- trust boundary is configured with **mls qos trust cos | dscp** command

The following table summarizes the standard queuing techniques available:

Table 4-4 Standard Queuing Techniques

Priority Queuing	traffic assigned to queue is serviced and emptied first
FIFO	default hardware queuing (QoS disabled)
WFQ	assigns bandwidth based on weights to traffic flow
WRED	congestion avoidance to avoid queue tail drops
CBWFQ	assigns specific bandwidth to traffic classes

Compare Shaping and Policing

The following statements describe the supported features for shaping and policing. In addition the differences are noted as well.

- Policing does not queue packets
- Shaping does support packet queueing
- Policing is applied to ingress and egress interfaces
- Policing drops or remarks traffic that exceed CIR

There is no support for traffic shaping on ingress interfaces (egress only). In addition policing does allow access lists as a classification method.

Traffic Policing

Traffic policing allows you to control the maximum rate of traffic transmitted or received on an interface. Traffic policing is often configured on interfaces at the edge of a network to limit ingress and/or egress traffic. The standard configuration is to transmit packets less than or equal to CIR and drop or remark packets that exceed CIR.

The primary purpose of traffic policing is to provide multiple options for packet handling based on allowed data rate and burst rate. The conditions include conforming, exceeding and violating. The actions include forward, remark or drop. The following describe each condition and the action available.

> conforming = packet is forwarded or remarked
> exceeding = packet has exceeded limits and is dropped or remarked
> violating = data rate is faster than CIR and allowed, dropped or remarked

Note that remark can refer to either marking up or down of a packet. The network administrator could decide for instance to remark packet to a higher (preferred) DSCP marking in the Type of Service (ToS) field of an IP header.

Congestion Management

Congestion points where QoS is most recommended and crucial include aggregation uplinks and LAN to WAN transition.

The bandwidth assigned to the priority queue (PQ) is allocated whether the interface is congested or not. It works as a minimum bandwidth guaranteed to the assigned traffic class at all times. Packets assigned to the priority queue are discarded when the bandwidth is exceeded.

The bandwidth assigned to Class Based Weighted Fair Queues (CBWFQ) are used only when there is congestion. That allocated bandwidth is available to all traffic classes until then. In addition they are serviced (dequeued) only after the priority queue is emptied.

5.0 Infrastructure Services

5.1 Troubleshoot Client Connectivity Issues Involving DNS

The IOS command **ip name-server** configures the DNS server IP address for a Cisco network device. All DNS queries are sent to the DNS server resolve the IP address from a hostname. That enables Telnet hopping that is based on a hostname between network devices.

DNS servers resolve a known IP address to an unknown hostname. In addition they can resolve a known hostname to an unknown IP address. Connecting to web servers for instance is based on a domain name.

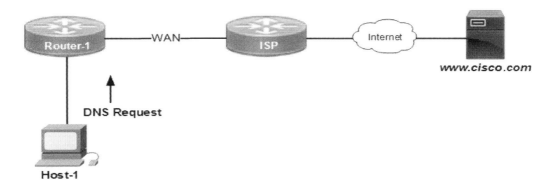

The following techniques are used to verify the DNS server is reachable and hostname resolution is working properly.

- ping www.google.com *(returns a request timed out error message if unavailable)*
- nslookup www.google.com *(verify IP address and domain name)*
- nslookup 127.0.0.0 [dns server ip address] *(host loopback to test DNS server)*

5.2 Configure and Verify DHCP on a Router

DHCP Server Configuration

router(config)# **ip dhcp pool** [name]
router(dhcp-config)# **network** [ip address range]
router(dhcp-config)# **dns-server** [ip address]
router(dhcp-config)# **default-router** [ip address]

The default lease time for an IP address assigned from a Cisco based DHCP server is 1 day. The routers and switches would renew the IP address after 24 hours when triggered by a host request.

The network address and broadcast address should not be included with the DHCP pool for dynamic assignment. The host assignment would include anything else unless it is statically assigned already.

The host IP address renewal is based on the lease time setting. The host will typically keep using the same IP address assigned. The lease renewal request is sent to the DHCP server when the lease time expires. The DHCP server will extend the lease again for the lease time interval setting.

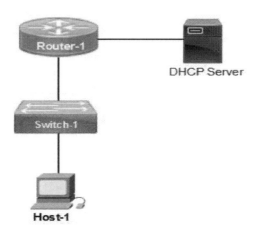

DHCP Relay

The IOS commands configure the DHCP relay agent for hosts on VLAN 10. There is support for assigning physical interfaces as well. The **ip helper-address** command is configured with the IP address of the DHCP server. All DHCP requests arriving from hosts are forwarded to the DHCP server (172.16.3.1) on a remote subnet. The DHCP relay agent is the router configured with the **ip helper-address** command.

> router> **enable**
> router# **configure terminal**
> router(config)# **interface vlan 10**
> router(config-if)# **ip helper-address 172.16.3.1**

Verify DHCP Bindings

DHCP binding table is comprised of entries with host IP address and MAC (hardware) address. That could include any network devices and servers configured as DHCP client. Cisco routers and switches can provide DHCP services to enabled hosts. The following IOS command lists the bindings for all DHCP enabled hosts.

> router# **show ip dhcp binding**

IP Address	Hardware Address	Lease Expire	Type
172.16.1.1	0000.000a.aaaa	Aug 16 2017 17:00 PM	Auto

Troubleshooting DHCP

Layer 3 connectivity is verified with a ping of the DHCP server IP address. The cause of DHCP address assignment is often configuration errors on the DHCP server. In addition configuring DHCP server with the wrong DHCP relay address will cause errors.

DHCP uses Ping or Gratuitous ARP to detect IP address conflicts. The DHCP server will **ping** the proposed IP address to confirm it is not assigned. The ICMP echo reply is sent from any network device or host if it is already in use. The DHCP server will log the conflict error with a Syslog server. That is enabled with the **ip dhcp conflict logging** feature as a default.

Gratuitous ARP (GARP) is sent by a router as well to detect IP addresses in use. The network device would reply with an ARP to confirm IP address is not available. The DHCP server removes any IP address from the DHCP pool until conflicts are resolved.

router# **show ip dhcp conflict**

IP Address	Detection Method	Detection Time
172.16.1.32	Ping	July 16 2017 9:30 AM
172.16.1.64	Gratuitous ARP	July 16 2017 10:30 AM

The following command lists current DHCP pool status on the router. That includes the range of assigned IP addresses, number of leased addresses and any pending events. Misconfigured DHCP server causes various Layer 3 connectivity issues. That includes incorrect host subnet mask, default gateway address and DNS server address.

router# **show ip dhcp pool**

Utilization mark (high/low)	: 100 / 0
Subnet size (first/next)	: 0 / 0
Total addresses	: 254
Leased addresses	: 142
Pending event	: none

1 subnet is currently in the pool:

Current index	IP address range	Leased addresses
10.10.1.1	*10.10.1.1 - 10.10.1.254*	142

Verify Host DHCP Settings

The host command to list all IP addressing is **ipconfig /all.** It provides the current TCP/IP settings including IP address, DHCP server and DNS server address. In addition MAC address and default gateway address can be verified.

The Windows desktop command **ipconfig /release /renew** will release the current IP address and request a new IP address. The DHCP server would assign a random IP address from the pool along with additional settings.

5.3 Troubleshoot Client and Router-Based DHCP Connectivity Issues

The DHCP server is responsible for dynamic configuration of host IP settings. In addition it manages the renewal of new IP addresses from an address pool.

DHCP address pool is defined on the DHCP server along with the lease time period. The DHCP address pool is a range of IP addresses reserved for dynamic assignment for hosts. The host could receive default gateway and DNS server addresses as well.

Host DHCP Request

The DHCP request for an IP address starts with server discovery. The DHCP server replies with an IP address lease offer. The host replies with an IP lease request for the proposed IP address. The DHCP server confirms the IP address with a lease acknowledgement to the host. The DHCP server will send the lease time and any additional address settings as well. The following are standard DHCP message types.

> Step 1: Server Discovery = DHCPDISCOVERY
>
> Step 2: IP Lease Offer = DHCPOFFER
>
> Step 3: IP Lease Request = DHCPREQUEST
>
> Step 4: IP Lease Acknowledgement = DHCPACK

5.4 Configure, Verify and Troubleshoot Basic HSRP

HSRP Operation

- HSRP advertises a virtual IP address to enable seamless failover to a standby router. The virtual router is based on a shared virtual IP address and MAC address. That enables redundancy for fast failover to the standby router.

- The active HSRP active router is assigned the virtual IP address and MAC address for packet forwarding. The standby router is assigned the virtual addressing when the active router isn't available. HSRP virtual IP address is the default gateway for hosts on the common subnet. VRRP is the open standard equivalent FHRP to HSRP.

- The virtual IP address assigned to the HSRP group is configured on both router members with the **standby 1 ip** command. The group number and virtual IP address are assigned to the HSRP routers.

- HSRP is not a routing protocol and virtual IP address is not installed in the routing table. It is a default gateway address where packets are forwarded for routing services.

- Hello packets are sent between active and standby router at 3 second intervals by default to detect neighbor state. In addition the hold timer is 10 seconds.

The default HSRP values include the following settings:

- Hello timer = 3 seconds
- Hold timer = 10 seconds
- Standby priority = 100
- HSRP version = HSRPv1
- Enabled groups = none
- Default group = 0

HSRP Groups

The virtual MAC address for version 1 is **0000.0c07.ac01**. This is for the group 1. The rightmost 2 bits (01) indicate the group number. The default HSRP group 0 would be assigned virtual MAC address **0000.0c07.ac00** for version 1.

There is support for assigning a maximum 255 groups per physical interfaces or VLAN interfaces. Multiple groups across multiple routers enable configuration of load balancing. At least one HSRP group is associated with at least two routers.

Priority Setting

The default HSRP priority is 100. The active router is configured with a higher priority than standby router. The router with the highest IP address is elected the active router when all priorities are equal.

HSRP provides a tracking feature that detects when the active HSRP router is not available. That triggers a failover to the standby router. The priority of the active router is decremented by **10** as a default. The standby router has a higher priority and becomes the active router.

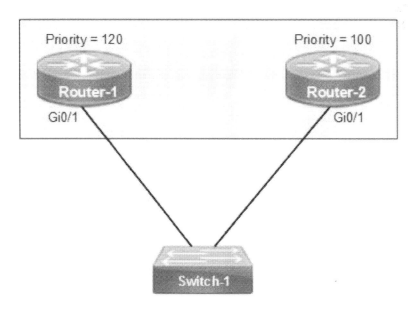

Preemption

The **preempt** command enables comparison of priority between routers to elect an active HSRP router. It is configured on all HSRP enabled routers so the router with highest priority becomes active. The following command configures a local interface as standby so that it becomes active when the current active router fails.

> router(config-if)# **standby 1 preempt**

Version

The following are virtual MAC addresses based on the HSRP version.

- HSRPv1 = 0000.0c07.acxx
- HSRPv2 = 0000.0C9f.fxxx
- HSRP for IPv6 = 0005.73a0.0000 through 0005.73a0.0fff

HSRP version 2 sends hello messages to multicast 224.0.0.102 address. There are additional features supported with HSRPv2. The number of groups available with HSRPv2 is 4096 (0-4095) and IPv6 addressing is supported as well.

HSRP Configuration

> router-1(config)# **interface gigabitethernet0/1**
> router-1(config-if)# **ip address 172.16.1.1 255.255.255.0**
> router-1(config-if)# **standby version 2** *(enables HSRPv2)*
> router-1(config-if)# **standby 1 preempt** *(compare router priorities for group 1)*
> router-1(config-if)# **standby 1 priority 110** *(active router)*
> router-1(config-if)# **standby 1 ip 172.16.1.3** *(virtual IP address)*

Verify HSRP

The following IOS command displays the HSRP operational status for all groups. The status includes active router, standby IP address, virtual addressing and timers.

> router# **show standby**

Troubleshooting HSRP

The virtual IP address must be assigned from the same subnet as the router interfaces. All timers must match between HSRP router peers. The HSRP version must match between routers as well. There are features enabled with HSRPv2 not supported with HSRPv1. The VTP modes for both routers must match. The active router configured as VTP server requires the same VTP mode for standby.

HSRP States

The valid HSRP states from the list include Standby, Init and Active. In addition there is Listen and Speak states.

1. *Initial (Init)*: This is the start state indicating that HSRP isn't running.

2. *Learn*: The virtual IP address is unassigned and no hello message was received from the active router yet.

3. *Listen*: The virtual IP address and MAC address is known by the router. The active and standby router is unassigned. It listens for hello messages from HSRP enabled routers.

4. *Speak*: The router sends hello messages to elect active and standby router.

5. *Standby*: The router is in standby mode and monitors hello packets sent from the active router. It becomes active when active router fails.

6. *Active*: The router forwards packets to the HSRP group. In addition the active router sends regular hello packets.

5.5 Configure, Verify and Troubleshoot Inside Source NAT

Network Address Translation (NAT) translates private IP addressing to a public routable IP address for outbound internet traffic. The inbound traffic from the internet is translated (mapped) to a private IP address.

The following are primary advantages of NAT

- conceals private IP address assignments from the internet
- eases management of internet connectivity

The disadvantage to NAT is the IP address renumbering when switching internet service providers (ISP). The public routable (internet) IP address is used to configure translation for any static or dynamic NAT configuration.

Static NAT

The static NAT translation is a 1:1 configured mapping between local and global addresses. The static translation manually assigns a private IP address to a public IP address. For instance, three public routable IP addresses will allow three static NAT translations. As a result they are a permanent entry in the NAT translation table. They enable a remote host connection from an outside (external) network.

Dynamic Pool

Dynamic NAT pool mapping translates each private IP address to an available public IP address (1:1) in the NAT pool. The dynamic NAT pool of public IP addresses is shared by all internal IP addresses on a first come first served basis. The maximum number of simultaneous internet connections available is limited to the number of public IP addresses in the NAT pool.

Port Address Translation

Port Address Translation (PAT) is an IP address translation technique that translates the most internal (private) IP addresses to a single or multiple public IP addresses. It is an enhancement to NAT that assigns a unique source port number to each translated IP address. The host IP address for instance could be identified with 200.200.1.1:10 as the translated source IP address. The 10 is the unique source port making the translated IP address unique. The 16 bit source port field allows for translating 65,535 private (internal) IP addresses to a public IP address. There is support for a pool of addresses or single interface.

192.168.1.1:10 ⟶ 200.200.1.1:10

192.168.1.2:11 ⟶ 200.200.1.1:11

192.168.1.3:12 ⟶ 200.200.1.1:12

The following IOS command enables Port Address Translation. The **source list 1** points to ACL 1 that permits a range of internal (private) IP addresses to be translated. The [pool name] refers to a NAT pool that has a single or multiple public routable IP addresses assigned. The **overload** keyword enables port address translation of multiple internal IP private addresses to a single public IP address.

router(config)# **ip nat inside source list 1 pool** [pool name] **overload**

NAT Addressing

Inside Local IP Address (172.16.1.1/24)
Private IP address assigned to a host on the inside network (RFC 1918).

Inside Global IP Address (172.33.1.1/24)
Public internet routable IP address assigned by the ISP.

Outside Global IP Address (200.200.1.2/24)
Public internet routable IP address assigned to outside (remote) host device.

Outside Local IP Address (200.200.1.2/24)
Public internet routable IP address of outside host as appears to inside network.

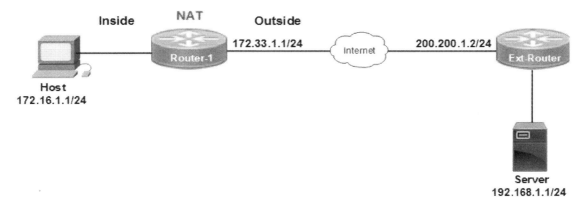

NAT Configuration

The following configuration creates a NAT public pool of 10 public addresses. That is assigned for translating a range of private host addresses. In addition the overload feature is enabled for port address translation. The alternate to **netmask** keyword is **prefix-length 28** that assigns the same /28 subnet mask (255.255.255.240).

1. Assign NAT inside interface

> R1(config)# **interface fastethernet2/0**
> R1(config-if)# **ip nat inside**
> R1(config-if)# **exit**

2. Assign NAT outside interface

> R1(config)# **interface fastethernet1/0**
> R1(config-if)# **ip nat outside**
> R1(config-if)# **exit**

3. Create a NAT pool **cisco** and assign <u>ten</u> public addresses from the range 172.33.1.1 to 172.33.1.10 (*subnetting rules apply here*)

> R1(config)# **ip nat pool cisco 172.33.1.1 172.33.1.10 netmask 255.255.255.240**

4. Create access-list 1 to permit private host range 192.168.1.10 to 192.168.1.40 (*wildcard mask rules apply here*).

> R1(config)# **access-list 1 permit 192.168.1.9 0.0.0.7**

5. Assign access control list 1 to the NAT pool and enable the overload feature.

> R1(config)# **ip nat inside source list 1 pool cisco overload**

Verify NAT

The following command verifies network address translation is working correctly.

> R1# **show ip nat translations**

5.6 Configure and Verify NTP Operating in Client/Server Mode

The following table matches time source on the left with description on the right.

Table 5-1 Cisco Network Device Time Sources

ntp peer	backup time server
system calendar	initializes software clock after restart
software clock	initially set by hardware clock
ntp server	external time server

The following are all correct statements concerning NTP network protocol.

- provides time source for logging and time stamp transactions
- N+1 server redundancy (NTP master + NTP failover server)
- reference is UTC coordinated universal time
- DNS is required for resolving time server IP address
- stratum level is the distance from the NTP authoritative time source

The following statements correctly describe NTP operation:

- server mode routers provide time source to client mode devices
- time servers are hierarchical
- server mode routers poll an external time server

The **ntp master** command configures a network device as an NTP reference clock source. It is alternative to an external authoritative time source and not recommended.

Configure NTP

The following IOS command configures an external time server as authoritative time source for a router.

router(config)# **ntp server 172.16.1.1**

Verify NTP

The following IOS commands are used to verify NTP server synchronization status, time source activities and stratum level for a router.

router# **show ntp status**
router# **show ntp associations**

110

6.0 Infrastructure Security

6.1 <u>Configure, Verify and Troubleshoot Port Security</u>

Static

Switch ports configured with port security only accept frames from addresses that have been dynamically learned or manually configured. The switch port enabled with port security would deny access based on an unknown MAC address. Port security default setting is to allow only one MAC address per switch port.

Dynamic

The following IOS command enables port security on an access switch port. The MAC address of the connected host is learned dynamically and added to the MAC address table. The MAC address persists in the switch table until the switch is powered off. In addition the MAC address is deleted from the MAC address table when the host is disconnected from the switch.

> switch(config-if)# **switchport port-security**

Sticky

The following statements describe primary characteristics of port security.

- The *sticky* keyword adds dynamically learned addresses to the running configuration script.

- The sticky MAC addresses do not age out of the MAC address table.

- The switch does have to relearn the MAC addresses after every reboot unless the running configuration is saved to startup configuration file.

- Removing the *sticky* keyword causes dynamically learned the MAC addresses to persist in the MAC address table only for the connected session

> switch(config-if)# **switchport port-security** *(enables port security)*
>
> switch(config-if)# **switchport port-security mac-address sticky** *(add MAC address 0000.000a.aaaa to running configuration)*
>
> switch(config-if)# **switchport port-security maximum 1** *(1 device only)*

Max MAC Addresses

The following port security interface commands prevent connecting a hub or any second device to a shared switch port.

> switch(config-if)# **switchport mode access**
> switch(config-if)# **switchport port-security maximum 1**

Violation Actions

The four configurable violation modes include protect, restrict, shutdown and shutdown VLAN. The switch interface can add up to the maximum number of allowed MAC addresses to the address table.

The security violation is triggered when there is an attempt from a host with a MAC address not in the MAC address table. Duplicate MAC address error causes a violation as well. The restrict mode causes the switch to drop all packets from an unknown source. SNMP trap alerts are sent, syslog messages are logged and the violation counter is incremented. Protect mode only sends a security violation notification.

The following 802.1X switch port states occur when there is a security violation.

- restrict
- errdisable

Errdisable Recovery

The following IOS global configuration command will re-enable a switch port interface in err-disable state caused by a port security violation. The default setting is to re-enable the port with **shutdown** and **no shutdown** interface configuration commands.

> switch(config)# **errdisable recovery cause psecure-violation**

Verify Port Security

Each of the following IOS commands can verify port security is configured on a switch port interface. In addition **show port-security** interface command provides status information.

> switch# **show port-security interface gigabitethernet 1/1**
> switch# **show running-config**

6.2 Describe Common Access Layer Threat Mitigation Techniques

802.1X Port-Based Authentication

802.1X authentication is an open standard supporting multi-vendor network devices. It is an IEEE protocol that authenticates hosts requesting network access. User authentication of clients is enabled from switch ports where there is public access.

The RADIUS server authenticates a username and password. In addition there is MAC authentication bypass available. The host MAC address is used as the username and password for identity.

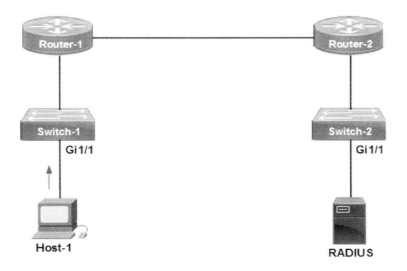

Cisco port security is hardware (MAC) based authentication. It controls the MAC address/s allowed and number of devices. The following correctly describe the features of 802.1X port-based authentication:

- prevent unauthorized hosts from connecting to network
- RADIUS based user authentication
- supports MAC address authentication
- monitor mode collects and analyzes authentication requests

The host connected to an 802.1X enabled switch port waits for an EAP request/identity frame from the switch. The client can initiate authentication by sending EAPOL-start frame if the EAP request/identity frame isn't sent.

The following are three common causes for 802.1X authentication to fail.

- host (client) does not have 802.1X compliant software
- host (client) MAC address is not permitted
- no connectivity to RADIUS server

The following IOS command enables 802.1X with switch-side authentication.

switch(config-if)# **authentication port-control auto**

The following IOS show command will list the authorized state of an 802.1X client along with host mode and timer configuration.

switch# **show dot1x interface** [interface-id] **details**

The data VLAN and voice VLAN must be assigned to a separate VLAN ID. That is required for connecting a Cisco IP phone to an 802.1X enabled switch port.

DHCP Snooping

DHCP snooping is a security feature that acts like a firewall between untrusted hosts and trusted DHCP servers. The following are services provided by DHCP snooping:

- permit DHCP packet types to trusted ports only
- prevent rogue DHCP servers from offering IP addresses to hosts

DHCP snooping feature is enabled both globally per network device and per VLAN. The network administrator would enable snooping on VLAN/s assigned to switch access ports and **trunk uplink connected to the router**. Typically the hosts VLANs are configured for snooping. For DHCP snooping to work properly, all DHCP servers must be connected to the switch through trusted interfaces. In addition all untrusted DHCP messages are forwarded only to trusted interfaces.

The following statements are true of a switch trusted interface:

- DHCP snooping trust interfaces are enabled on a Layer 2 Ethernet interface or port channel to forward all DHCP broadcast messages.

- Trusted interface must have Layer 3 reachability to DHCP servers.

- The switch uplink is typically enabled as a DHCP trusted interface for that purpose. That provides connectivity to the router for packet forwarding to DHCP servers on remote subnets.

DHCP Snooping Configuration

switch(config)# **ip dhcp snooping** *(enables globally)*
switch(config)# **ip dhcp snooping vlan 10** *(enable snooping on vlan 10)*
switch(config)# **interface gigabitethernet1/1** *(uplink to router)*
switch(config-if)# **ip dhcp snooping trust** *(configures interface as trusted)*

Configure switch ports with DHCP clients (hosts) as untrusted with **no ip dhcp snooping trust** interface level command.

114

Nondefault Native VLAN

The native VLAN is used to forward untagged packets across a switch trunk. Management traffic STP and DTP are always sent across native VLAN. The default native VLAN is assigned to VLAN 1. That is the same as the default management VLAN for switches. The native VLAN should not be assigned to VLAN 1 to prevent security or STP issues. As a result assigning a Nondefault native VLAN is a security best practice.

The following are correct statements for the nondefault native VLAN:

- native VLAN must match between connected switches
- forwards untagged packets (STP and DTP) across a switch trunk
- native VLAN for switch trunk port should not be assigned the default VLAN 1

The following command configures a Nondefault native VLAN 999 instead of the default VLAN 1. It is configured on all switch port interfaces assigned as trunk ports. Note that control traffic CDP, PAgP and VTP is always forwarded across VLAN 1

switch(config-if)# **switchport trunk native vlan 999**

6.3 Configure, Verify and Troubleshoot IPv4 and IPv6 Access Lists

Standard ACL

There are some recommended best practices when creating and applying access control lists (ACL). The network administrator should apply a standard access list closest to the destination. The standard access list is comprised of a source IP address and wildcard mask. It is very general and can inadvertently filter traffic incorrectly. Applying the standard access list near the destination where filtering is required prevents possible over filtering. The standard access list allows for only specifying a source address and wildcard mask. The wildcard mask is used for filtering purposes.

Extended ACL

The extended access list should be applied closest to the source. The extended access list is granular (specific) and filters traffic based on stringent requirements. It includes source address, destination address, protocols and port numbers. Applying an extended access list closest to the source prevents traffic that should be filtered from traversing the network. That conserves bandwidth and additional processing required at each router hop from source to destination.

Some access control lists (ACL) are comprised of multiple statements. The ordering of statements is key to the ACL working as expected. The router starts from the top (first) and cycles through all statements until a matching statement is found.

The packet is dropped where no match exists. The network administrator should order ACL statements from most specific to least specific. Assigning least specific statements first will sometimes cause a match to occur with an ACL that wasn't intended for that packet. As a result the match on the intended ACL statement never occurs.

The more specific ACL statement is characterized by source and destination addresses with shorter wildcard masks (more zeros). In addition protocols and port numbers are often specified. The first ACL statement is more specific than the second ACL statement. There is an implicit **deny any any** statement added to the end of each ACL.

> permit tcp 192.168.1.0 0.0.0.255 host 10.10.64.1 eq 23
> deny tcp any any eq 23

Example 1:

The Cisco ACL for IPv4 and IPv6 use similar syntax from left to right. For instance the ACL reads as - *deny tcp traffic from host address (source) to host address (destination)*. All web-based applications are TCP-based and as such requires **deny tcp**. The **eq www** specifies the TCP-based application to deny.

> reads as - *deny http from host 2001:0:AD03::1 to 2001:34F:20DC:24DE::1F*

The **deny tcp** with no application specified will deny traffic from all TCP applications (Telnet, FTP, SSH etc). It would however allow all UDP-based application traffic. The **deny ipv6 host** command when configured won't allow UDP or TCP traffic. IP is a lower layer protocol and required for higher layer protocols.

Example 2:

Refer to the network topology drawing. What ACL statements are required to configure the following security requirements?

> deny telnet traffic from 10.0.0.0/8 subnets to Router-2
> deny http traffic from 10.0.0.0/16 subnets to Router-2
> permit any traffic not matching

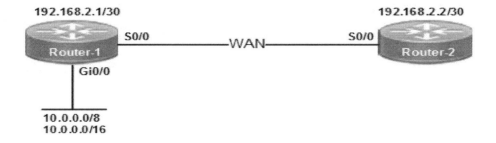

The following IOS commands will configure the correct ACLs based on the security requirements:

    router(config)# **access-list 100 deny tcp 10.0.0.0 0.255.255.255 any eq 23**
    router(config)# **access-list 100 deny tcp 10.0.0.0 0.0.255.255 any eq 80**
    router(config)# **access-list 100 permit ip any any**

The other options have either a wrong wildcard mask, application port number or no **permit ip any any** statement. All extended access control lists must have a permit all source and destination traffic with **permit ip any any** as a last ACL statement.

The other options have either a wrong wildcard mask, application port number or no **permit ip any any** statement. All extended access control lists must have a permit all source and destination traffic with **permit ip any any** as a last ACL statement.

The following examples describe syntax for source and destination ports. Note that hosts in the context of ACLs refer to desktop, server or network devices. Configuring both ACL statements would filter traffic from the source and to the source as well.

        permit tcp **any any** eq 80
        Allows all traffic with destination port 80 (http) from **any** host to **any** destination

        permit tcp **any** eq 80 **any**
        Allows all traffic with source port 80 (http) from **any** host to **any** destination

Applying ACL to Router Interface

The ACL must be applied to an interface for it to inspect and filter traffic. In addition the *in | out* keywords specify the direction to filter packets at the interface. The *out* keyword applies ACL rules to all outgoing traffic on an interface. The *in* keyword applies ACL rules to all incoming traffic on an interface.

The ACL is applied with interface level IOS command **ip access-group 100 out**. The ACL is removed with **no ip access-group** command from the interface.

The **ip access-group in | out** command refers to an ACL by name or number. The **access-class in | out** command filters VTY line access only. There is only one access list that can be applied inbound or outbound per interface per layer 3 protocol

The output from **show ip interface** command lists the ACL, interface and direction.

Named ACL

Named ACLs are similar to extended ACLs and allow for dynamically adding or deleting ACL statements without having to delete and rewrite all lines. There is of course less CPU utilization required as well. They are easier to manage and enable troubleshooting of network issues.

Dynamic ACL

The dynamic ACL provides temporary access to the network for a remote user. The ACL configured defines the type of access permitted and the source IP address and timeout value for network access. It is designed for instance to permit a contractor or remote user temporary access to network services

IPv6 ACL Support

The following are three primary differences between IPv4 and IPv6 support for access control lists (ACL).

- IPv6 supports only named ACLs
- IPv6 permits ICMP neighbor discovery (ARP) as implicit default
- IPv6 denies all traffic as an implicit default for the last line of the ACL

Proper ACL operation requires **permit ipv6 any any** (all traffic) as a last statement to permit any traffic not matching an ACL. In addition it prevents all traffic from being blocked when there are no ACL permit statements.

The ACL sequence number determines the order of inspection and where any new ACL is added in the list. The new ACL is added to bottom of the list when no sequence numbers are specified

Verify ACL

The following IOS command lists all IPv4 ACLs configured on a router.

router# **show access-lists**

The following IOS command lists all IPv6 ACLs configured on a router.

router# **show ipv6 access-list**

Troubleshooting ACLs

- missing **permit ip any any** statement
- incorrect order of statements
- incorrect application port number
- incorrect interface or direction applied

6.4 Verify ACLs Using APIC-EM Path Trace ACL Analysis Tool

Path Trace (PT) is a feature available with Cisco APIC-EM that can identify the exact path between two endpoints. The trace is determined based on the endpoint IP addresses and a 5-tuple description for a flow. This helps automate inspection and enable cost effective faster troubleshooting. The following are correct statements concerning Path Trace:

- endpoint support for hosts and/or layer 3 interfaces
- enable automated network troubleshooting
- identify redundant and shadow ACL rules

Network discovery is required before starting ACL Path Trace. In addition SSH or Telnet is required to enable APIC-EM controller access to the devices. The network discovery feature collects information on devices and builds an inventory database.

ACL Path Trace analyzes how a flow is affected by any ACLs deployed on the path. After the path between source and destination is calculated, the ACL Trace analyzes both ingress and egress interfaces of all devices on the path. The analysis is cumulative per ACL and not end-to-end path.

The following are correct statements concerning ACL Path Trace operation:

- Path is calculated between endpoints (source and destination IP address)

- ACL Path Trace analyzes how a flow is affected by ACLs deployed on the path and for troubleshooting ACL issues.

- Cisco ACL Path Trace is supported on layer 3 interfaces only

6.5 Configure, Verify and Troubleshoot Basic Device Hardening

Local Authentication

The following IOS command will configure a username called *cisconet* with user EXEC mode privilege. In addition the password for the manually configured account is *cisco*. The same command is used on Cisco Catalyst switches and routers. Privilege level 15 is the highest privilege level and level 1 (user EXEC mode) is the lowest.

device(config)# **username *cisconet* privilege 1 password *cisco***

Hidden Password

The following IOS command will configure a username called *admin* with privilege level 15 and a hidden password. The 7 designates the password as hidden (encrypted) with the configuration script. The encrypted password is copy/pasted to the command line.

The **service password-encryption** command must be enabled on the network device for type 7 encryption.

    device(config)# **username *admin* privilege 15 password 7** [encrypted password]

Enable Password

The following IOS commands will configure an enable password on a Cisco switch or router. The enable password will be required before access to privileged EXEC mode is allowed (switch#). That mode then allows access to global configuration mode.

    device> **configure terminal**
    device# **enable**
    device(config)# **enable password cisco**

Line Console

The following commands will assign password *cisco* to the switch or router console port. Any login attempt to the console port will require that password.

    device(config)# **line console 0**
    device(config-line)# **password *cisco***
    device(config-line)# **login**

Service Password-Encryption

The purpose of **service password-encryption** command is to encrypt passwords in the running and startup configuration scripts. It applies to all passwords except secret passwords. It makes device passwords unreadable for security purposes. That includes authentication key, enable, console, VTY and BGP neighbor passwords. It does not however encrypt secret passwords.

The following IOS command is used to encrypt all plain-text passwords on a Cisco device. The passwords are encrypted in the running configuration and startup configuration script.

    router(config)# **service password-encryption**

Secret Password

The following IOS command will configure a username called ***admin*** with privilege level 15 and a hidden secret password. The 5 designates the password as secret and hidden (encrypted) with the configuration script.

    device(config)# **username admin privilege 15 secret 5** [encrypted password]

The secret encrypted password is copy/pasted to the command line. It is common to copy the encrypted password from another network device. Secret passwords are based on MD5 hash algorithm that is uncrackable making them more secure than type 7 passwords. In addition the secret password is encrypted automatically and do not require service password-encryption.

Access to Network Devices

VTY Lines

The following IOS commands will enable Telnet login, configure password *cisco* and timeout value of 5 minutes for the default VTY lines (0 4). Note that an enable password must be configured on the device as well for Telnet to work correctly.

device(config)# **line vty 0 4**
device(config-line)# **password** *cisco*
device(config-line)# **login**
device(config-line)# **exec-timeout 5**

Login Local

The IOS command **login local** enables the use of the local database for VTY line access. The username and password is manually configured in the local device database for user authentication. The same IOS command is used to configure console access as well. Any AAA server configuration with TACACS or RADIUS takes precedence over any login local when configured.

device(config-line)# **login local**

Device Management Protocols

The following IOS command allows only SSH protocol traffic inbound to the default VTY lines (0 4). It will deny all other protocols inbound access to the VTY lines including Telnet. The Cisco default is to allow all protocols inbound and outbound access.

device(config-line)# **transport input ssh**

The following describe usage of the **transport** command to filter protocols. The **input | output** keyword determines whether inbound or outbound traffic is permitted with the default to allow all inbound and outbound traffic.

device(config-line)# **transport input all** (default) = allow all protocols (telnet, ssh etc.)
device(config-line)# **transport input telnet ssh** = allow Telnet and SSH only

The following password types are encrypted:

- SSH session password
- password type 7
- enable secret password

Login Banner

The following IOS command configures an MOTD banner for a Cisco device.

device(config)# **banner motd** ^ enter text ^

6.6 <u>Describe Device Security Using AAA with TACACS+ and RADIUS</u>

The AAA security model includes authentication, authorization and accounting.

- authentication verifies user identity for approving access to the server
- authorization allows user access to applications and data on the server
- accounting provides audit trail of transactions for security analysis and forensics

The following is a list of disadvantages with using AAA server authentication:

- AAA server is a single point of failure
- local account is required as a backup on network devices
- same AAA password is used for multiple network devices

The following table lists characteristics and features supported with AAA server types.

Table 6-1 AAA Server Characteristics

TACACS+	Cisco proprietary
RADIUS	multi-vendor open standard
TACACS+	TCP
RADIUS	UDP
TACACS+	separates authentication, authorization and accounting
RADIUS	integrates authentication and authorization
TACACS+	encrypts all communication
RADIUS	encrypts passwords only

The following are three advantages of TACACS+ over RADIUS server.

- TACACS+ supports 15 privilege levels
- TACACS+ enables controls for user authorization levels
- TACACS+ allow for device administration

TACACS+ is a server-based authentication protocol that allows defining of authorization policies per group. As a result TACACS+ is well suited to managing the access security for thousands of network devices.

RADIUS is limited to privilege mode with network access and authentication only.

- Wireless authentication
- 802.1x port-based authentication

The user will often complain that access to a particular network device is not available. The following command will verify the login access for AAA user account is disabled.

    device# **show aaa local user lockout**

Local AAA

The local AAA authentication method will use the local username and password database configured on the router.

The IOS command **aaa authentication login default local** enables AAA authentication to use the device local username database. There is an option as well to configure local authentication as failover for AAA as well.

7.0 Infrastructure Management

7.1 <u>Configure and Verify Device-Monitoring Protocols</u>

SNMPv2

SNMP is a network management protocol that enables monitoring of network device. The following are three components that enable SNMP communication.

- MIB
- SNMP Manager
- SNMP Agent

The Cisco network device will send all enabled notifications to the SNMP server. Enabling a lot of SNMP MIBs can cause high CPU utilization on Cisco devices. The number of queries (polling) increase with the MIBs enabled. The problem worsens particularly with polling of routing and ARP tables

The authentication type used by SNMPv2 is community strings. The following IOS command configures an SNMP community string named **cisco** with read/write access.

> device(config)# **snmp-server community *cisco* rw**

The following IOS command will configure an SNMP server named ***nms.cisco.com*** with version 2c and enable trap messages.

> device(config)# **snmp-server host *nms.cisco.com* traps version 2c**

SNMPv3

The following three features are enhancements available with SNMPv3.

- message integrity
- authentication
- encryption

The following are authentication protocols used by SNMPv3.

- HMAC-MD5
- HMAC-SHA

Alert messages generated by SNMPv3 agents include both ***Trap*** and ***Inform***. The purpose of Trap messages is to send alerts to the network management station. The network device sends a Trap to the NMS alerting that a network interface status is down. The Inform message is an acknowledgement of a Trap to confirm it arrived.

The following are correct statements concerning the features of SNMPv2 and SNMPv3.

- SNMPv3 provides security enhancements
- SNMPv2 added the Inform protocol message to SNMP
- SNMPv2 added the GetBulk protocol message to SNMP

The following command configures an SNMP server with IP address of 172.16.1.1 and enables SNMPv3. In addition there is MD5/SHA authentication for optimized security.

router-2(config)# **snmp-server host 172.16.1.1 version 3 auth**

Syslog Server

The following are correct statements concerning Syslog server utilization.

- Syslog provides granular messaging to support enterprise SNMP architecture.
- Syslog provide a scalable solution for storing messages on an external server.
- Syslog is an effective solution for managing logs and is disabled by default.

The traps are logged to the Syslog server. The default logging trap level for Syslog messages is to receive informational (6) and lower messages except debugging messages (level 7). Configure **logging trap** [level] command to change the default on Cisco network devices.

The following IOS command enables forwarding of system messages on a Cisco network device to a Syslog server.

device(config)# **logging 172.16.1.10**

7.2 Troubleshoot Network Connectivity with ICMP Echo-Based IP SLA

The following two statements are correct concerning ICMP echo-based IP SLA.

- IP SLA responder is not required on the destination device
- monitors hop-by-hop response time (network latency)

7.3 Configure and Verify Device Management

The default number of simultaneous Telnet sessions supported by a Cisco router is five. They are comprised of the default VTY lines 0 4 (0,1,2,3,4)

The following command restore the startup configuration file from TFTP server.

device# **copy tftp: nvram:startup-config**

The following command is used to backup the startup configuration file from network device to TFTP server.

     device# **copy nvram:startup-config tftp:**

Startup Configuration

The following describes what the Cisco network device does when no startup configuration file is found during bootup:

1. The Cisco network device first attempts to load the startup configuration from NVRAM (default location). There is a copy made of the startup configuration loaded to DRAM for active use. That is referred to as the running configuration.

2. The network device attempts to load the startup configuration file from TFTP server if there is no startup configuration in NVRAM.

3. The network device starts the initial configuration dialog mode if there is no configuration to a TFTP server or it is unavailable. That enables a start from scratch configuration. The preferred method is to restore the most recent startup configuration where available.

     --- System Configuration Dialog ---

     Would you like to enter the initial configuration dialog? [yes/no]: **yes**

Deleting the startup configuration and restarting the network devices will put the network interfaces in shutdown state. Entering **no shutdown** command on Router-1 Gi0/0 and Router-2 Gi0/0 interfaces will enable CDP between the devices.

Feature Licensing

Cisco feature set licensing is based on feature packages. Each package bundle include additional protocols and enhancements from the default *ipbasek9* package. Encryption protocols such as IPsec and SSH require the *securityk9* feature license upgrade.

Logging

The logging facility default setting is *local7* for switches and routers.

- Emergencies (level 0)
- Alerts (level 1)
- Critical (level 2)
- Errors (level 3)
- Warnings (level 4)
- Notifications (level 5)
- Information (level 6)
- Debugging (level 7)

Time Zone

The following global IOS commands assign hostname *switch-1* and configures *PST* timezone for the switch. Hostnames cannot start with a number or have any spaces.

> switch(config)# **hostname switch-1**
> switch-1(config)# **clock timezone PST -8**

Loopback

The loopback interface is virtual and always available when there is at least one physical interface up. Routers have at least two physical interfaces. The loopback interface is unaffected by issues with any single interface. The router cannot be managed when a physical interface assigned for management purposes is unavailable. The following example is typical of a loopback interface configuration. The standard subnet mask for a loopback is a /32 host mask.

> router(config)# **interface loopback0**
> router(config-if)# **ip address 192.168.254.254 255.255.255.255**
> router(config-if)# **end** *(return to privileged exec mode)*

7.4 <u>Configure and Verify Initial Device Configuration</u>

Console Settings

The Cisco network devices provide a console port for direct connection from a laptop. It is typically used for initial configuration and troubleshooting purposes. The following are default settings for the Cisco console port interface.

- 9600 bps, 8 data bits, 1 stop bit, no parity, no flow control

Cisco Device Modes

The following table correctly match the Cisco device modes and prompts:

Table 7-1 Cisco Device Modes and Prompts

user EXEC mode	device >
enable mode	device#
privileged EXEC mode	device(config)#
rommon mode	rommon >
routing configuration mode	router(config-router)#

The **show running-config** command is used to verify any changes that were made before saving the running configuration.

>   device# **show running-config**

Network Management SVI

The following IOS commands configure a management IP address (SVI) for a layer 2 switch. The Cisco recommended best practice is to assign an unused VLAN for remote switch management. The default VLAN 1 is used to forward control traffic (CDP, VTP, PAgP) between switches.

>   switch(config)# **interface vlan 100**
>   switch(config-if)# **ip address 172.16.1.254 255.255.255.0**
>   switch(config-if)# **no shutdown**

The following IOS command will save the running configuration changes to the startup configuration file:

>   device# **copy running-config startup-config**

The alternate IOS command used is the following:

>   device# **copy system:running-config nvram:startup-config**

The following IOS command allows the network administrator to run IOS show commands from global configuration mode.

>   device(config)# **do** [show command]

The following command provides a list of all active users connected to the VTY lines.

>   device > **show users all**

The following IOS command displays CPU utilization for a Cisco device.

>   device# **show process cpu**

Show Version

The output of **show version** command lists the current IOS code version along with feature set license. The **show version** command is also available from user mode prompt. The **show version** command the following operational status.

- configuration register settings
- amount of Flash and DRAM memory available
- most recent router power cycle (reboot) method used

7.5 <u>Perform Device Maintenance</u>

IOS Upgrades, Recovery and Verify (SCP, FTP, TFTP, MD5)

The following table describes file transfer methods for copying IOS image and configuration files:

Table 7-2 Cisco File Transfer Methods

FTP	server-based, username and password logon, TCP
SCP	adds encryption (SSH), supports larger files
TFTP	server-based, not secure, UDP, single connection
USB	fast, network device slot, local copy

IOS Upgrades

The IOS image file is stored in Flash memory on Cisco devices. The Flash memory is permanent non-volatile file storage. On bootup the IOS image is loaded from Flash to DRAM volatile memory. The startup configuration is stored in permanent non-volatile NVRAM. The running configuration is the startup configuration file loaded to DRAM.

Before doing any IOS upgrade to a Cisco device it is important to verify available device memory. The IOS image file will requires a minimum amount of Flash memory based on file size. In addition there is a minimum amount of DRAM required to boot the IOS image as well. The minimum required Flash/DRAM memory is listed with each IOS filename. The **show version** command will list the amount of available Flash and DRAM memory on the Cisco network device. The following is an example of output from **show version** for router Flash memory usage (bytes).

[73400320 bytes used, **195035136 available**, 268435456 total]

The total Flash memory installed is 256 MB. The Flash memory used by files including the current IOS is approximately 70 MB including any additional files. That leaves approximately **186 MB available** for any new IOS with the original IOS image left on Flash. Compare the IOS image file size from cisco.com with the available Flash memory. The IOS upgrade from TFTP server has a copy dialog prompt to delete IOS image on flash

TFTP Server

TFTP server support is available for managing IOS images and startup configuration files. It is an alternative to using memory on the network devices for storing files. Cisco supports loading IOS and startup configuration file from TFTP server at bootup as well.

130

Access to the TFTP server is only required at bootup to download files. The following are recommended actions before doing an IOS image backup to TFTP server.

- create directory on TFTP server with security access.
- verify disk space available on TFTP server.
- configure access to TFTP server from ROMmon mode.

The following IOS command will copy the IOS image file to Flash memory.

device# **copy tftp: flash:**

The following command verifies the integrity of IOS image file on Flash memory.

device# **verify /md5** [filesystem: filename]

Selecting IOS Image on Bootup with Default Configuration

1. The device starts and does Power on Self Test (POST) to verify all hardware is operational. The bootstrap loader then determines where to load the IOS image based on the configuration register settings. The default setting loads the first IOS listed with any **boot system** command in the router startup configuration file. The **boot system**   command points to a location of an IOS image stored in Flash memory. The file location configured with the first **boot system** command is used when multiple commands exist.

2. The first IOS image listed in Flash memory (where multiple IOS images exist) is loaded when there are no **boot system** commands.

3. IOS is loaded from TFTP server when there is no IOS image on Flash.

4. ROMmon mode starts when there is no IOS image on TFTP server.

Standard locations where a router can load an IOS image

- TFTP
- Flash
- ROM

Configuration Register

The network device starts Power On Self Test (POST) to run diagnostic software from ROM and verify all hardware is operational. The router examines the configuration register value that specifies where to load the IOS. The default value of the configuration register is *0x2102*.

Configuration Register Settings:

0x2100: Boot from ROM only.

0x2101: Use the first IOS listed in Flash and ignore any boot system command.

0x2102: Load the IOS image based on the location specified with the boot system command configured in startup configuration file. Load IOS from Flash if no boot system command is configured. Load the startup configuration file from NVRAM. Ignore the break key and boot to ROM mode if boot fails. (default setting).

0x2142: Ignore break key, boot to ROM mode if boot fails and ignore the startup configuration file.

The default configuration register setting is *0x2102*. That causes the Cisco device to load the IOS image file specified with the **boot system** command. The following IOS command assigns the IOS image filename to use for bootup. It is a global configuration mode command.

> router(config)# **boot system flash**: [IOS filename]

Password Recovery and Configuration Register

The following is the correct order for performing password recovery on a Cisco router or switch from the local console port.

Step 1:	Reboot router and press Ctrl-Break key to start ROMmon mode
Step 2:	Modify the configuration register to prevent the startup configuration file from loading: rommon > **confreg 0x2142**
Step 3:	Reboot router and issue the following IOS command: router# **copy startup-config running-config**
Step 4:	Change the password and save changes with the following IOS command: router# **copy running-config startup-config**
Step 5:	Modify the configuration register with the following IOS command: router(config)# **config-register 0x2102** and reboot.

File System Management

There are two options available for erasing the startup configuration and restarting a switch or router.

> Option 1:
>
> device# **erase startup-config**
> device# **reload**

> Option 2:
>
> device# **write erase**
> device# **reload**

Cisco devices store the startup configuration file in NVRAM. The IOS command **erase nvram:** will delete all files from NVRAM including startup configuration. That will cause the initial configuration dialog mode to start when the device is reloaded. The IOS command **erase startup-config** will only delete the startup configuration file instead of all files on NVRAM.

The following IOS command will list the Flash directory on a Cisco device.

> device# **dir /all**

The following IOS command will delete a file from Flash memory. Include any specific subdirectories for the file location where applicable as well.

> device# **delete flash:**[filename]

7.6 Use Cisco IOS Tools to Troubleshoot and Resolve Problems

Ping

The **ping** command will verify layer 3 connectivity from the source interface where it was issued to a destination interface. That is accomplished with a ping of the remote host IP address. Ping sends ICMP echo requests and receives echo reply messages. The default source interface for the **ping** command is the egress interface IP address.

The following statements are true of the **ping** command.

- Extended ping is used to determine the type of connectivity problem.
- Extended ping tests network latency performance.

The following command is used to verify that an IPv4 or IPv6 interface is responding

> router# **ping** [ip address]

Extended ping allows for specifying a variety of parameters for troubleshooting purposes. Examples includes number of packets, source interface and packet size.

Traceroute

The Cisco version of **traceroute** is based on sending 3 UDP datagrams to each hop between source and destination hosts. ICMP packets contain messages that are encapsulated within the IP layer 3 header. The TTL field of the UDP datagram is incremented by one with each hop that isn't the destination.

The following statements describe the use of **traceroute** for troubleshooting purposes.

- Traceroute verifies the path packets take in order to get to a destination.

- Traceroute can troubleshoot routing issues including routing loops and packet filtering (ACL or firewall).

The **traceroute** command on a Cisco device allows you to view hop by hop packet routing of traffic. The output of **traceroute** lists each Layer 3 hop IP address hop taken from source to destination.

> router# **traceroute** [destination ip address]

The **tracert** command is only available from the Windows command line. The trace is from the desktop source IP address instead of switch or router interface.

Terminal Monitor

Cisco devices do not send log messages to a terminal (VTY) session as a default. The VTY lines are used for Telnet and SSH sessions. The following IOS command enables terminal logging to send log messages to the terminal. That includes debug output and system error messages.

> device# **terminal monitor**

Log Events

The following statements correctly describe Cisco terminal logging.

- Telnet/SSH logging messages to the VTY terminal is disabled by default.
- Console logging messages is enabled by default.

Local SPAN

Local SPAN is comprised of source and destination interfaces on the same switch. The SPAN copies traffic from source interface/s to a destination interface where a network analyzer is attached. There is support for either multiple source interfaces or a single VLAN.

There are at least two source interfaces defined. The hosts that are connected have established a network session. The trunk source interface copies traffic from all VLANs.

The following IOS commands will configure Local SPAN on a Cisco switch.

> switch(config)# **monitor session 1 source interface Gi1/1**
> switch(config)# **monitor session 1 destination interface Gi1/2**

The following is a description of Local SPAN components:

Table 7-3 Local SPAN Components

source port	interface or VLAN
destination port	interface
forwarding traffic	transmit, receive or both
Local SPAN	source and destination port on same switch

7.7 Describe Network Programmability in Enterprise Network Architecture

The following statements correctly describe SDN programmability:

- SDN architecture decouples the control and data plane
- control plane is a software module instead of a physical processor
- SDN controller is a centralized control plane with a policy engine
- infrastructure is abstracted from applications

The following statements accurately describe the SDN Controller:

- centralized management and network intelligence
- network services are dynamically configurable
- network appears as a single switch
- moves control plane from physical devices to software abstracted layer

The following statements correctly describe the purpose of SDN APIs:

- SDN applications requests are sent via northbound APIs
- SDN Controller relays information via southbound APIs to network devices
- APIC-EM is the Cisco SDN Controller

CCNA IOS Show Commands

The following is a list of the most common IOS commands associated with questions from the CCNA exam. They are all standard IOS commands used to configure, verify and troubleshoot network connectivity. The IOS commands are based on all topics from the published CCNA exam guidelines.

CCNA CLI Help Facility

Mode Level

The List of commands available from each Cisco device mode is available with question mark **?** from each top level mode prompt.

        rommon > **?**
        switch > **?**
        switch# **?**
        switch(config)# **?**
        switch(config-if)# **?**

Command Level

The command level **?** provides a list of all commands for that subgroup such as show commands for instance. In addition the question **?** after any IOS command displays syntax options for that specific command. It is a quick reference for correct configuration syntax and commands not supported with the current IOS version.

        switch# **show ?**
        switch(config)# **vtp mode ?**
        switch(config-if)# **?**
        switch(config-if)# **show interfaces ?**

Partial Commands

The partial command level question **?** provides a list of all commands that begin with the letters specified. That helps list commands available that start with the same letters.

        switch# **c?**

Global Commands

show running-config

Display the current running configuration script on any Cisco device.

show version

Display a variety of device information including the following:

- IOS version
- license feature set
- configuration register setting
- hardware

show protocols

Verify operational status (up/up), IP address and subnet mask of all network interfaces.

show ip interface brief

Summarizes the operational status (up/up) and IP address of all switch and router interfaces. The *Status* column is equivalent to *Interface* (Layer 1) for show interfaces command. The *Protocol* column is equivalent to *Line Protocol* (Layer 2) for show interfaces command.

show interfaces *[interface]*

Display the operational status (up/up), IP address, configuration settings and errors for a specific switch or router interface.

- operational status
- speed
- duplex
- MTU
- interface errors

show cdp

Verify that CDP is enabled, update timer, hold timer and CDP version.

show cdp neighbor detail

Display all directly connected neighbor devices and confirm there is Layer 2 connectivity to each neighbor and the following neighbor details:

- local interface
- neighbor hostname
- neighbor interface
- neighbor IOS version
- neighbor hardware platform

show lldp

Verify that LLDP is enabled and timer settings.

show lldp neighbors detail

Display all multi-vendor neighbors directly connected to a Cisco device and confirm there is Layer 2 connectivity to each neighbor.

- local interface
- neighbor hostname
- neighbor interface
- neighbor IOS version
- neighbor hardware platform

show memory

Display the total, used and available memory on a Cisco device.

show process cpu

Display the CPU utilization for a Cisco device at five minute intervals.

show environment

Verify the operational status of fans, temperature and power supplies. In addition list the percentage of power supply utilization and what amount is available.

do [show command]

Run show commands from any device mode prompt.

LAN Switching Technologies

show vlan brief

Display all configured VLANs, verify active status and any switch ports assigned.

show vlan

Display all configured VLANs, verify active status and any switch ports assigned. There is some additional VLAN information provided as well.

show interface switchport

Display the operational mode and administrative mode for local switch ports and enable status. In addition there is a variety of trunking configuration and VLAN pruning information.

show interfaces trunk

Verify the operational status of trunk interfaces and list configuration settings:

- switch port members
- allowed VLANs
- native VLAN
- encapsulation type
- trunk mode

show interfaces status

Display the Layer 2 *connected / notconnect* status for each switch port and configuration settings.

- connected / not connect
- interface speed
- duplex settings
- VLAN
- Ethernet standard

show interfaces [interface] transceiver

Display the Layer 1 characteristics of the transceiver connected to a switch port interface.

show etherchannel summary

Verify all EtherChannel links configured on the local switch including the operational status.

- operational status
- channel group number
- negotiation protocol (PAgP/LACP)
- switch ports assigned

show interface port-channel [number]

Verify the operational status (up/up), configuration and errors for a port channel interface assigned to an EtherChannel.

- IP address
- speed
- duplex
- MTU
- interface errors
- port members

show spanning-tree vlan [number]

Display the spanning tree information for a specific VLAN.

- root bridge
- timers
- STP port types (local interfaces)
- port path cost

show spanning-tree interface [interface]

Display the spanning tree information for a specific switch interface.

- STP port type
- STP port state
- port path cost
- STP timers

show spanning-tree

Display the bridge ID for the local switch and root bridge ID for each VLAN including priority and timer settings.

- local bridge ID, priority and timers
- root bridge priority per VLAN
- root bridge MAC address per VLAN
- priority and path cost for local switch ports

show spanning-tree summary

Display the spanning tree protocol enabled on the local switch.

- spanning tree protocol enabled
- root bridge ID for each VLAN
- STP enhancements (PortFast etc.).
- STP port states per VLAN

show vtp status

Display various configuration information for the VTP domain where the local switch is a member.

- version number
- configuration revision
- operating mode of local switch
- domain name

show mac address-table

Display MAC address, port number and VLAN of each host connected to the local switch.

Routing Technologies

***ping** [ip address] [hostname]*

Confirms Layer 3 network connectivity between a source and destination based on sending and return of ICMP packets.

***traceroute** [ip address] [hostname]*

Confirm the routing path for Layer 3 connectivity between a source and destination based on UDP packets.

show ip route

Display the routing table for the local router that includes all known subnets, routing protocol, next hop address, metrics and administrative distance. In addition the gateway of last resort (default route) is shown when it is configured.

show ip arp

Display the IP address and MAC address bindings in the router ARP table. The MAC address of servers and network devices are learned through ARP requests and added to the local cache.

show ipv6 interface brief

Verify the operational status (up/up) and IPv6 address for all router interfaces.

***show ipv6 interface** [interface]*

Verify the operational status (up/up), IPv6 addressing, configuration settings and errors for a router interface.

- speed
- duplex
- MTU
- interface errors

show ip protocols

Display a variety of settings and configuration for all enabled routing protocols on the router.

show ip ospf

Display various configuration settings for each OSPF process enabled on the router.

- router ID
- timers
- interfaces per area
- area range (subnet)

142

show ip ospf neighbor

Verify all OSPF adjacencies established with directly connected OSPF neighbors.

- neighbor router ID
- IP address
- adjacency state
- assigned DR/BDR

show ip ospf interface [interface]

Verify the operational status (up/up) of an OSPF enabled interface. In addition Display the OSPF configuration for the interface.

- IP address
- area assigned
- process ID
- router ID
- network type
- timers
- assigned DR/BDR
- adjacent neighbor

show ip ospf database

Display the OSPF link state database topology that includes Link State Advertisements (LSAs) for all OSPF neighbors advertising from all areas.

- link state advertisements
- advertising router
- process ID
- router ID

show ipv6 ospf interface [interface]

Verify the operational status (up/up) of an OSPF for IPv6 enabled interface. In addition list the IPv6 addressing and OSPF configuration for the interface.

- IPv6 address
- area assigned
- process ID
- network type
- timers
- assigned DR/BDR

show ipv6 ospf neighbor detail

Display all OSPFv3 for IPv6 adjacencies established with OSPF neighbors.

- neighbor router ID
- IPv6 addressing
- adjacency state
- assigned DR/BDR

show ip eigrp neighbors

Display all EIGRP adjacencies established with directly connected EIGRP neighbors.

- neighbor IP address
- local interface
- autonomous system number
- hold time
- SRTT, RTO and queue count

show ip eigrp interfaces

Display all active EIGRP interfaces associated with an autonomous system (AS).

show ipv6 eigrp neighbors

Display all EIGRP for IPv6 adjacencies established with directly connected neighbors.

- neighbor IPv6 address
- local interface
- autonomous system
- hold time
- SRTT, RTO and queue count

show ipv6 eigrp interfaces [interface]

Verify all active EIGRP for IPv6 interfaces associated with an autonomous system (AS).

show ip eigrp topology

Display all successor and feasible successor routes to a destination in addition to DUAL states.

show ip rip neighbors

Display all active sessions the local router has established with RIPv2 neighbors that include neighbor IP address and interface.

WAN Technologies

show interfaces multilink *[interface]*

Display the IP address and encapsulation type for the multilink interface.

- operational status (up/up)
- interface errors
- LCP / IPCP negotiation status

show ppp multilink

Verify the multilink interface status as enabled for the router.

- bundle name
- local and remote hostnames
- member interfaces
- packet errors

show pppoe session

Display all PPP over Ethernet (PPPoE) sessions enabled for the router.

- local and remote MAC address of peers
- local interface
- dialer number

show ip bgp neighbors

Display all BGP neighbor peering sessions established and TCP connection information. The neighbor configuration includes the following.

- router ID
- IP address
- neighbor feature capabilities

show ip bgp summary

Display all BGP routing information for the neighbor connections including prefix (subnet), attribute and prefix (subnet) information.

show interface tunnel *[number]*

Verify the operational status (up/up) of the tunnel and the assigned IP address. In addition the tunnel source address and local interface is shown along with transport configuration.

Infrastructure Services

show ip dhcp conflict

Display all IP address conflicts detected on the IOS DHCP server when allocating IP addresses to DHCP clients.

show ip dhcp binding

Display the IP address and MAC address of DHCP client, lease expiration and assignment type on the IOS DCHP server.

show ip dhcp snooping

Verify that DHCP snooping is enabled along with assigned VLANs and interfaces configured for snooping. In addition verify the VLANs are operational for snooping.

show standby

Display the HSRP configuration on the local router for the router group configured.

- virtual IP address
- virtual MAC address
- timers
- active router
- standby router

show ip nat translations

Verify the NAT addressing assigned for translating between private and public addressing.

Infrastructure Security

show port-security interface *[interface]*

Display the port security configuration for a switch interface.

show dot1x interface *[interface]* *details*

Display the switch side settings for port-based authentication of a host.

show access-lists

Display all IPv4 access control lists configured on the local router to verify filtering of packets.

show ipv6 access-lists

Display all IPv6 access control lists configured on the local router to verify filtering of packets.

Infrastructure Management

show ntp status

Verify the synchronization status to an NTP peer, IP address of NTP peer, local stratum level and clock signaling.

show users all

Display all inbound connections to the local device including VTY, console and AUX lines.

show terminal

Display terminal settings for the current terminal line and transport protocols allowed for remote management access (SSH, Telnet etc.)

show flash

List the files currently on flash memory including available memory.

erase nvram:

Delete all the files on NVRAM including the startup configuration.

show logging

Verify the logging configuration and where it is enabled/disabled on the network device. In addition list all error messages logged for a specific device

Host Commands

ipconfig /all

Verify the network connectivity status, IPv4/IPv6 addressing and MAC address for a host. In addition the DNS servers and DHCP configuration are listed.

arp -a

Display the contents of the local ARP cache.

tracert [ip address] [hostname]

The host version of traceroute command to verify routing path from the host.

nslookup [domain name]

Confirm DNS server is working correctly.

Printed in Great Britain
by Amazon